AZTEC RUINS
ON THE
ANIMAS

University of New Mexico Press
ALBUQUERQUE

AZTEC RUINS
ON THE ANIMAS

Excavated,
Preserved, and
Interpreted

By
Robert H. Lister
and
Florence C. Lister

Library of Congress Cataloging-in-
Publication Data

Lister, Robert Hill, 1915–
  Aztec ruins on the Animas.

  Bibliography: p.
  Includes index.
  1. Aztec Ruins National Monument
(N.M.)
  2. Pueblo Indians—Antiquities.
  3. Pueblos—New Mexico.
  4. Indians of North America—New
Mexico—Antiquities.
  5. Excavations (Archaeology)—New
Mexico.
  6. New Mexico—Antiquities.
  I. Lister, Florence Cline.
  II. Title.
E99.P9L52 1987   978.9′82
86-30748
ISBN 0-8263-0925-9
ISBN 0-8263-9026-7 (pbk.)

Contents

PREFACE

This volume documents in words and pictures the excavation and preservation of the Aztec Ruins, a major Southwestern archaeological site in the San Juan Basin of northwestern New Mexico. The original investigation was undertaken during the infancy of archaeological endeavors and exemplifies the turn from indiscriminate collecting of "objects of antiquity," for monetary gain or personal gratification, to scientific inquiries directed toward creating a better understanding of the way of life of the aboriginal inhabitants of the area and a desire to protect and preserve significant archaeological remains for the benefit of future generations.

Earl Morris is an integral part of the story. Born and raised in the vicinity of Aztec Ruins, educated at the University of Colorado, he devoted many years of his pioneering efforts in Southwestern archaeology to the excavation and preservation of the Aztec Ruins. At the time of his field work, there were few established models or techniques to guide him. Archaeology was a new

and evolving science. Still, the methods Morris followed in digging and the interpretations he drew from the old pueblo, its inhabitants, and the artifacts he recovered have stood up fairly well in light of more recent archaeological investigations and advances in technology.

In our treatment we generally have followed Morris's interpretations of the evidence he observed or collected as stated in the reports Morris prepared for the American Museum of Natural History, the institution that sponsored his excavations. These explanations of life and events at Aztec and its two sequential occupations: first, by people possessing a culture similar to that of the Chaco Canyon folk to the south, and then by emigres from the north exhibiting a Mesa Verde life-style, still are the basis for the National Park Service visitor interpretive program at Aztec Ruins National Monument today.

Most archaeologists have accepted Morris's points of view and have repeated or expanded them in numerous current publications. Recently, however, a few archaeologists have proposed new interpretations of old and recent data that question some of the oft repeated suppositions about Aztec. These controversial views are still being tested and debated and whether they ever will replace the ideas first put forth by Earl Morris remains to be seen. We have chosen to side with the traditionalists until the fate of the newer explanations is determined by the archaeological community.

The recognition of Aztec as an outlying community and a key installation in a widespread integrated economic, social, and ritual system centered in Chaco Canyon has evolved in the last ten years as a result mainly of a reexamination of the ruins of Chaco Canyon and adjacent regions by teams of National Park Service archaeologists and environmentalists.

If our compilation of prose and photographs about Aztec Ruins and the individuals and organizations who have contributed to its excavation, preservation, and interpretation prove of some benefit to visitors to Aztec Ruins National Monument or to those of the general public interested in archaeology, our purpose in preparing this volume will have been fulfilled.

We consider the captioned photographs in this work to be as important as the written segments. Together they form the text. Of particular significance are the pho-

tos taken by Earl Morris during the excavation of the West Ruin and the reconstruction of the Great Kiva. We are extremely grateful to the University of Colorado Museum, Boulder, Colorado, for permission to reproduce a selection of them herein. Other photographs kindly were provided by the National Park Service's Western Archeological and Conservation Center, Tucson, Arizona, and Chaco Center, Albuquerque, New Mexico; the Southwest Parks and Monuments Association, Tucson, Arizona; Aztec Ruins National Monument, Aztec, New Mexico; and Jerry Jacka, photographer of Phoenix, Arizona. In addition, our thanks are extended to the following individuals who generously provided much appreciated assistance in numerous ways: Joe Ben Wheat and Frederick Lange, University of Colorado Museum; Mark Sawyer, photographer, and the staff of the library and archives, Western Archeological and Conservation Center; Tom Windes, Chaco Center; Clarence Gorman, Superintendent, and his staff, Aztec Ruins National Monument; Carolyn Dodson, Southwest Parks and Monuments Association; and Elizabeth C. Hadas, Director, and Claire Sanderson, Editor, University of New Mexico Press.

Robert H. Lister
Florence C. Lister

AZTEC RUINS
ON THE
ANIMAS

In the absence of many other diversions, a
trip to the ruins on the west terrace of the
lower Animas valley was a favorite pas-
time. Such excursions provided many
photo opportunities, such as this scene
taken in the standing upper walls of the
north wing of the West Ruin. Courtesy
University of Colorado Museum.

CHAPTER ONE
The Ruins Discovered

Nineteenth-century America, a nation of ethnic diversity, longed for a native New World lore to which it could secure its anchorless cultural grappling irons. Surprisingly, many of its citizens found such an anchor in a factual, erudite 1840s account of the rise of the Aztec Empire of central Mexico and its audacious defeat some three centuries before by a small band of intrepid Spanish soldiers.

Just as this book, *The Conquest of Mexico* by William Hinkling Prescott, was at the height of its unanticipated popularity, a few prehistoric ruins in the Southwest, most notably those of Chaco Canyon some 150 miles west of Santa Fe, were becoming known to Americans as exploration of newly acquired former Spanish and Mexican holdings was undertaken. It was virtually inevitable that at first blush these ruins were attributed to either the Aztecs or their predecessors the Toltecs, whose own legends, as recorded in Prescott's book, had them emerging from some obscure origins in an ill-

defined northland. The prevalent fascination with the drama of Mexican history was further reflected in a score of place names that sprouted on maps of the West around the time of the Civil War. For example, in 1864 the first capital of the Arizona Territory, Prescott, was named for the recently deceased author of the lurid tale of the rise and fall of the Aztecs. Three of its dusty rutted streets were grandly christened Montezuma, Cortez, and Marina, for the Aztec emperor who was defeated by the Spaniards, the Spanish conqueror, and his Indian mistress.

Given this attitude, it is not surprising that in the 1870s as settlers inched south out of the central Rockies to the plateau leading toward the Colorado River and encountered long-abandoned vestiges of former occupations, they unhesitatingly regarded these ruins as signs of the northern domain of the vanquished Aztecs. The Utes, Navajos, and Apaches in whose modern range these antiquities lay were summarily dismissed as being too barbaric ever to have created the large and small house compounds whose crumbled remains were peppered in mounds across mesas and canyons. This cultural blind spot likewise prevented the Anglo migrants from suspecting any connections to the Pueblo Indians still living in numerous villages in the northern parts of the territories of Arizona and New Mexico. So it was that the large cluster of pre-white remains on a western terrace of the Río de las Animas Perdidas, or River of Lost Souls, in northwestern New Mexico, came to be known as Aztec Ruins. That left future culture historians the interminable task of explaining to the public that the Aztecs had never lived in New Mexico and that the Aztec Empire did not come into existence until several centuries after the site named in their honor had run its course.

Its name quickly shortened by the Americans to Animas, the river which lured settlers out of the mountains carried a large, fast-flowing volume of water constantly being replenished by the melting snows of the rugged, lofty San Juans, which punctuated the northern horizon. As it cut a southerly path along a relatively narrow valley bottom banked with rich alluvium, the river descended through a zone transitional from alpine lushness to barren, high tablelands engulfed in wild silence. Dark green cedars and piñons gave way to a tangle of deciduous growth at water's edge. At the point where the channel swung toward the west

and merged with the larger San Juan River, which eventually flowed into the mightly Colorado, the valley widened appreciably. On each side low, bleached sand hills covered with worn, rounded river cobbles and a sparse blanket of sage and saltbrush formed a broad, protected pocket where, despite the mile-high elevation, early visitors felt fruits and vegetables would have an ample growing season and neither winter nor summer would be too severe for livestock.

To test this premise, in 1876 a half dozen families drifted down the Animas from Colorado mining camps to make new lives in the wilderness abutting the immensity of the stark Navajo country. Their settlement became Aztec, named after the ruins. The settlers, mindful that other farmers at some unknown time had been there before them, must have formulated haunting questions about the underlying reasons for prehistoric failures. That their predecessors had tried to manage the environment for their cultural benefit was evidenced by traces of two ancient irrigation ditches cutting off from the river to follow along the western escarpment toward the north side of the most promising grouping of mounds, those called the Aztec Ruins. Occasional flash floods spewing out of tributary arroyos exposed another form of prehistoric farming activity, rectangular bordered garden plots strategically placed to take advantage of seasonal runoffs.

The Aztec Ruins themselves were

six major and a comparable number of lesser, distinct, high, weathered heaps of consolidated building slag and drifted wind- and waterborne dirt that came to rest about them. One main complex of jagged, coursed, sandstone masonry walls thrust above a dense scrub growth covering the highest and most westerly prominence. It was obvious that large buildings of several stories height, in at least the West Ruin, had collapsed to bury themselves in their own substance. The accumulated wreckage encroached upon a considerable acreage which the farmers would have liked for agricultural uses, but its debris did prove to be a handy source for construction materials.

Considering its isolated location, word of the discovery of the site spread east remarkably fast, where it reached the ears of anthropologist Lewis H. Morgan. He may have been aware of a report made twenty years earlier by John S. Newberry, a geologist working for a government survey, who had described from an informant's account an abandoned settlement that could have been Aztec Ruins. At any rate, Morgan came to examine the remains on the Animas in 1878. From a scientific point of view, his study and subsequently published plans and descriptions perceptively related the ruins to those in Chaco Canyon, sixty miles south of the San Juan. For the local citizens, however, Morgan's findings were of no particular interest compared to the urgencies of clearing land, planting and nurturing crops, and

erecting homes and outbuildings. But that lack of interest was to be dispelled three years later when, while on a Saturday outing, the local school master and some of his male students made startling discoveries in the heart of the ruins.

Few things seem as totally forlorn as a house emptied of its onetime occupants and left to fall apart, the human sounds within its walls forever quieted, its hearths turned cold. As the youths noisily pushed through the mound's thickets up into the enveloping arms of roofless second-story rooms along the ruin's crest, their youthful imaginations conjured up ghosts of departed residents within the eerie walls. The teacher fell to his knees in a corner of one partially exposed room, scraping back hardened earth and stones from fallen walls until, down almost five feet, he uncovered a layer of juniper splints that comprised a ceiling above a horizontally laid set of small peeled pine-log roof beams. Calling for his hatchet, he chopped through the brittle wooden mass until a large opening was broken into the first-floor room below. Although to the boys it appeared a black dungeon whose acrid, musty odors warned of bats, rats, snakes, and spooks, they cautiously lowered themselves down a rope into a sizable masonry-walled, cellar-like space. Through its gloom they soon saw that the room was empty. Not one to be discouraged, the teacher then directed his charges in prying out stones from one of the walls to allow them entrance into the adjoining chamber. At first the candles the boys lighted would not burn because of lack of oxygen in this interior cell deep beneath the surface of the mound. Gradually air coming through the breach in the wall kept their candles lit enough to reveal drifts of ancient rubbish and, in a corner, a seated skeleton staring at them! The flesh had long ago disintegrated, but the undisturbed bones remained articulated by dried ligaments, creating a gruesome spectacle. Immediately the frightened youngsters turned to escape, but the teacher pressed on. As he kicked through the loose debris on the floor, his foot hit another skeleton. This one had been laid out on the floor with its knees flexed up against the chest and then tied up in a strip of fiber matting. Though deposited without the formality of a grave, the deceased had been honored with an offering of several pottery vessels. Astounded by this bizarre adventure, the boys returned to their homes, where curious fathers soon made their own plans for a search of the ruins.

In the course of the next few weekends men from surrounding farms reentered the ancient house mass on the northeastern end of the mound where the schoolboys had broken into the rooms and at the opposite northwestern corner. On the ground floor level they tunneled horizontally through a number of walls and piles of compacted trash. Avoiding areas filled with slumped building rubble where heavy digging would have been required, ultimately they broke into about twenty of the best-preserved rooms of the north flank of the pueblo. Most had age-darkened wooden ceilings still intact, and mud plaster dados were partially discernible. Many of the rooms were empty except for fine-grained dust and sand that had filtered down to the use-hardened dirt floors. After being forsaken as a domicile, one had served as a communal tomb where thirteen bodies had been laid to rest upon the floor, accompanied by an assortment of well-preserved baskets, sandals, cotton cloth, and matting, and items less susceptible to decay, such as pottery, stone implements, and shell and stone ornaments. The artifacts left by the living and those placed with the deceased, which generally were identical, were gathered up from the rooms explored and taken back to the farmhouses. From there, like most curios, they gradually were dispersed and forgotten. Some of the farmers' own evidence was left behind; later excavators found a crowbar and whiskey bottle that had helped them in their ransacking.

One puzzling trophy was a copper pot that obviously had been smashed when a burning roof beam crashed down upon it. Such an object would not have belonged to the aborigines of the area, who had no metal items other than a few tiny ornamental copper bells acquired through trade with Mexico. Nor had there been any known fires within the structure in the American period flagrant enough to have brought down roof timbers. The collector who purchased the pot presumed it to have been discarded by an unknown Spanish or Mexican traveler who had visited the site some time in the prior two and a half centuries—long after its abandonment. Some late eighteenth-century knowledge of the ruins of the ancient town is suggested by notations on a 1776 map of the Escalante-Domínguez expedition from Santa Fe to the Colorado River. The strange copper vessel came into the possession of Scott Morris in 1895 after he had settled in nearby Farmington and, together with his six-year-old son, Earl, had become interested in the antiquities about their home.

Although Aztec Ruins were the region's first major victim of white man's vandalization, most further despoliation was discouraged when the property was acquired in 1889 by John R. Koontz. Three years later he permitted Warren K. Moorehead of Phillips Academy, Andover, Massachusetts, to make a detailed reconnaissance of the ruins but not to dig.

In the next three decades dozens of indications of former human presence were found across the sweep of the Colorado Plateau of northern New Mexico and Arizona and southern Colorado and Utah. A small cadre of self-trained and formally schooled archaeologists slowly replaced the looters bent on pothunting for profit who had instigated the initial search for relics. However, the spectacular beauty and forbidding nature of much of the topography that provided a backdrop for many sites, the abundance and amazing quality of abandoned settlements, the fascination of naturally desiccated human remains and excellently preserved artifacts, the mysteries of identity and fate, and the presence of colorful Native Americans all combined to make exotic fodder for the fantasies of professionals and laymen alike. Up to the time of World War I an aura of acquisitive romanticism prevailed. But slowly site by site and season by season the factual replaced the fantastic as objective science gained the upper hand.

By then the prehistoric culture of the Colorado Plateau was regarded as an ancestral one to that of modern Rio Grande, Zuni, and Hopi Pueblo Indians. Archaeologists later were to dub it Anasazi, a word the Navajo use to identify the builders of the multitude of prehistoric hamlets, villages, and towns that dot their reservation. It was recognized that, out of a more or less common background, regional variations had evolved as that culture moved to a climax at some undetermined time before whites arrived in the area. South of the San Juan River these intensifications were centralized in the arid districts about Monument Valley in Arizona and Chaco Canyon in New Mexico and north of the river about the Mesa Verde uplifts of Colorado and the broken lands westward into Utah. The tangible cultural manifestations of the latter two regions, Chaco Canyon and Mesa Verde, seemed to overlap along the eastern reaches of the San Juan as it

The Museum's field station occupies the plot on the left of the National Monument. The large plot on the right has been purchased by the Museum and tendered to the United States of America as an addition to the National Monument. On the plot, A to F are unexplored ruins; G, the Aztec Ruin, formerly owned and excavated by the Museum; H, the Museum's field headquarters

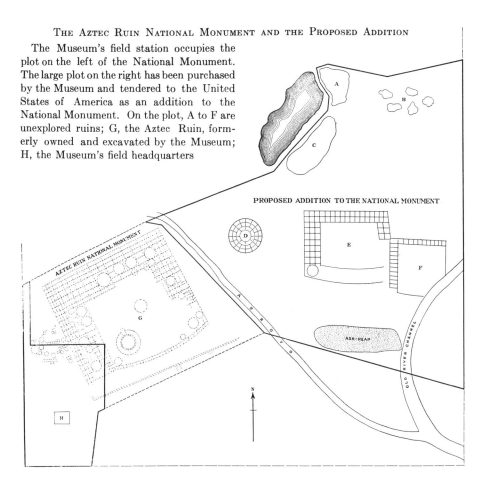

This figure is taken from an article on Aztec Ruins that appeared in the May–June 1927 issue of *Natural History*. It shows the original boundaries of the monument and the area added to it in 1928. The Museum's field headquarters, which contained the Earl Morris home, became part of the monument in 1930.

coursed from Aztec Ruins toward the Four Corners. This made study of the Animas site an attractive academic problem whose answers might help to elucidate past social and economic interactions and perhaps also contribute to an understanding of the causes for the eventual desertion of the territory.

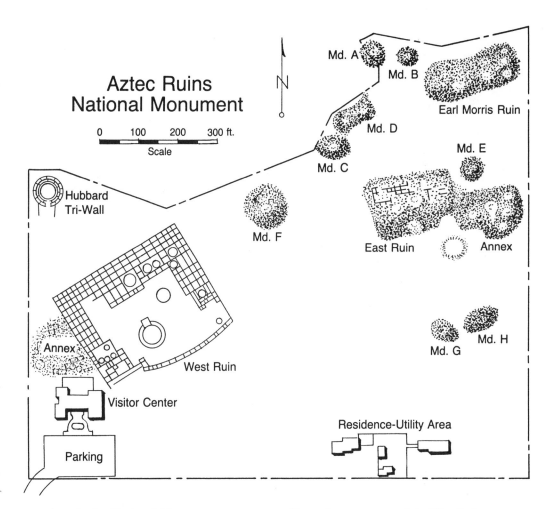

Aztec Ruins National Monument

0   100   200   300 ft.

Scale

Md. A
Md. B
Earl Morris Ruin
Md. D
Md. C
Md. E
Hubbard Tri-Wall
Md. F
East Ruin
Annex
Annex
West Ruin
Md. G
Md. H
Visitor Center
Residence-Utility Area
Parking

Aztec Ruins National Monument was established by proclamation of President Warren G. Harding on January 24, 1923 after the American Museum of Natural History donated 4.6 acres upon which most of the West Ruin was situated to the government. Subsequent additional donations by the American Museum of Natural History in 1928 and 1930 of a total of 14.4 acres, the purchase by the government in 1930 of 6.87 acres from the heirs of H. D. Abrams (the original owner of the entire site), and a donation of 1.25 acres by the Southwestern Monuments Association in 1948, brought the monument to its present size of 27.1 acres.

About three-quarters of the West Ruin was excavated by the American Museum of Natural History between 1916 and 1921; the Hubbard Mound, a tri-wall structure, was dug by the National Park Service in 1953 and subsequently partially backfilled for preservation of the feature. A few portions of the East Ruin have been examined, mainly in connection with stabilization measures. Limited explorations in Mound F indicate that it is likely another tri-wall unit. The Earl Morris Ruin and the remaining seven mounds within the monument boundaries are unexcavated.

As a youngster, Sherman Howe was in the group of schoolboys who in 1881–82 broke into ground-level rooms of the West Ruin. He returned later with the party of men who found the chamber with thirteen burials and many assorted artifacts. Sherman failed to share in the division of the find because of his age. Howe's father owned a farm just a half mile from the old settlement, so the ruins became a favorite place for occasional family outings. Over the years its jagged walls and hummocks of sand and rocks became thoroughly familiar to him. Therefore he eagerly joined the American Museum of Natural History crews when excavation of the site commenced in 1916. Howe returned in 1934 to participate in the restoration of the Great Kiva, partly because of his continued interest in the regional archaeology and partly to earn money to keep from losing his farm in the midst of the Great Depression. He and Morris had developed a firm bond of friendship through shared archaeological interests and because both their fathers had been pioneers in the settlement of the San Juan area. Morris credited Howe with expertise in masonry work, examples of which may be seen in the walls of the rebuilt Great Kiva.

Sherman Howe remained on his Animas valley farm until at the age of eighty and nearly blind, he moved to Oregon. However, before leaving the Animas valley, he recorded his experiences at the ruins. This photograph was taken in 1949. Courtesy University of Colorado Museum.

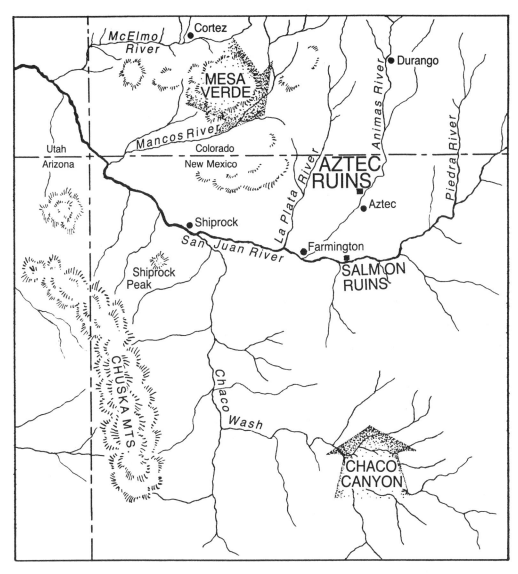

Map depicting Aztec Ruins in relation to the Chaco Canyon and Mesa Verde areas.

◁ The northwesternmost room of the ruin was one of those broken into by local citizens in 1881–82. The small breach they had made in its west wall was later enlarged into a rectangular doorway so that visitors to the site could easily enter this room and the contiguous rooms whose original ceilings were intact. Courtesy National Park Service.

The Ruins Discovered / 11

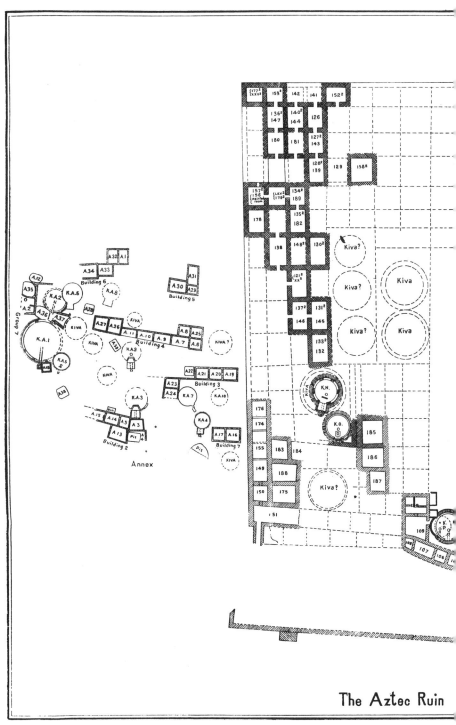

The Aztec Ruin

Earl Morris's 1923 map of the West Ruin as presented in his report, Burials in the Aztec Ruin, *Anthropological Papers of the American Museum of Natural History,* Vol. 26, Part 3 (1924): p. 145. A revised section of the map appeared in a later report, Notes on Excavations in the Aztec Ruin, *Anthropological Papers of*

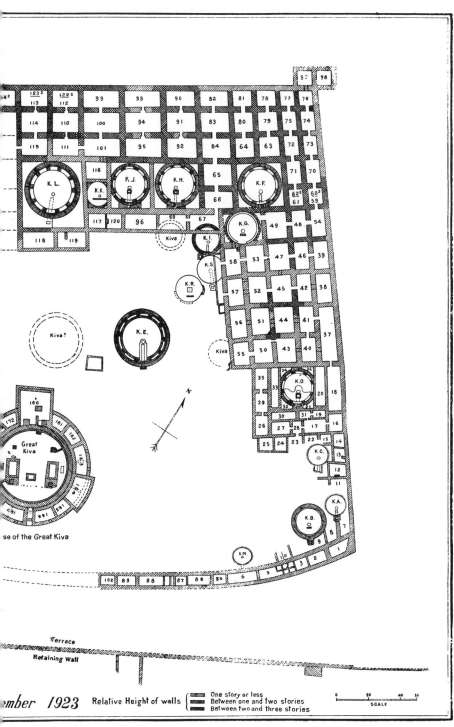

the *American Museum of Natural History,* Vol.
26, Part 5 (1928): p. 268. It identified a group
of rooms in the northwest sector of the ruin
that was cleared after publication of the 1923
map. Negative number 337597 (Photo by Earl
Morris). Courtesy Department Library Services,
American Museum of Natural History.

When first seen by early settlers in the Animas valley, the mounds they called the Aztec Ruins were covered with fallen wall and roof debris and accumulated earth. Scrubby growth grew on the elevations and crowded around the peripheries. This old photograph taken by Earl Morris in 1916 shows the exterior of the west wing of the house complex that would become known as the West Ruin. Several masonry walls are exposed, their height suggesting two stories in that part of the edifice. The piles of earth, beams, and the planking at the left end of the mound probably are remains of various early explorations made in that sector by local farmers. Courtesy University of Colorado Museum.

Once cleared of brush, the standing walls and mass of rubble of the ruins stood out in marked contrast to the intensely cultivated green valley bottom. This is a view from the north looking across the site toward the Animas River, and the village of Aztec hidden by trees is in the upper right. Courtesy University of Colorado Museum.

CHAPTER TWO

The Ruins Uncovered

EXCAVATION AND REPAIR

With the purpose of understanding the past, excavation of Aztec Ruins was undertaken from 1916 through 1921 in an agreement with a new owner, H. D. Abrams. The project was under the direction of Earl H. Morris, who had been engaged by New York's American Museum of Natural History to carry out the task. Funding came from museum patron Archer M. Huntington, whose fortune, derived from the Southern Pacific Railroad, had financed other early archaeological activities in the Southwest. The proposed two-pronged plan was to strip the entire West Ruin of its obscuring mantle of deposition and collapsed rubble in order to examine and recover whatever lay beneath it and to repair, but not restore, the uncovered structures so that they could withstand future weathering and public viewing.

The location of Aztec Ruins was unlike many of the larger ruins in the San Juan country. Rather than being tucked away on a remote, inaccessible cliff face or in a tract inhospitable to modern settlement,

the old town bulging up on a terrace above the river was a very familiar feature of the lower Animas landscape. Its rocky hummocks were an island encircled by the freshly plowed corn and alfalfa fields and apple orchards of an active community. Farmers' cows occasionally stumbled into the depressions of its structures. Sheep clambered along the craggy tops of its walls, loosening building stones as they went. Only a mile from the village that had grown up on the opposite bank of the river, it long had been a favorite spot to show visitors or to have family picnics. So, as work got under way, Morris was able to hire a crew of local farm hands. This freed him of the necessity of outfitting a field party with hand tools, camp gear, and foodstuffs, and assuming the expense and effort of transporting it all to some distant camp. Moreover, the men not only were accustomed to the hard physical labors and variety of mechanical skills involved but, like Morris himself, many had spent time digging in prehistoric debris and pondering its secrets. For their part, perennially hard-strapped farmers welcomed extra cash income. Perhaps most important of all was a rare proprietary community interest in the ruins which their proximity promoted. Many of the villagers came to witness the novelty of archaeological excavations.

In that formative period of the new science of archaeology, excavation, preservation, and interpretation techniques were still in their developmental stages. There were few tested guidelines to follow. Nowadays such a large-scale endeavor would not commence without mechanical earth-moving equipment and a body of specialists trained in computer analysis to contribute data and observations drawn from their areas of expertise. There would be a laboratory staff to process, repair, preserve, catalog, and photograph specimens. A team of experts in ruin stabilization would step in as unstable features were cleared. But Morris faced the responsibility of virtually singlehandedly salvaging the West Ruin domiciles and religious chambers from what he once called "the effacing hand of time" and ferreting out their place in the scheme of the Anasazi world, all the while making them secure for the future.

During the summers Morris was at the dig daily from sun up to sun down shoveling, brushing, exhuming, measuring, and photographing alongside the excavators. He directed the masons in needed reinforcements and helped set stone

walls and add cement capping. He cleaned and recorded artifacts, and he bought supplies and kept accounts. During the winters he prepared financial and progress reports for the museum, got notes in order, and plotted the next season's program. With all these year-round demands on time and energy, Morris never lost sight of the intellectual challenge posed by this great center of the ancients. When at last he had to quit because funds were depleted and the property had been purchased by the American Museum of Natural History and presented to the United States government, a third to a fourth of the ruin remained unexcavated. Morris wisely rationalized this disappointment as providing a necessary reserve for future testing with more advanced means.

Five reports upon various aspects of the research at Aztec were written by Morris and published by the American Museum of Natural History between 1919 and 1928. However, no detailed report was prepared on some categories of artifacts, many of which were already known from adjacent smaller habitations but some of which were rare and exceptionally well preserved. This was particularly unfortunate in the case of ceramics which served as his main criterion, other than architecture, in distinguishing between what he regarded as two distinct occupations of Chaco and Mesa Verde affiliated peoples. The pottery associated with a generalized Chaco background he considered Chacoesque or Chaco-like, but without full descriptions and illustrations, it now can only be assumed this meant a lesser product made along related lines. Neither did Morris have time nor money to dig thoroughly beneath the surface structures or central plaza to determine the precise extent of indicated earlier utilization of the same ground. Nevertheless, his prodigious efforts produced much new information and helped place the discipline of regional prehistory on a far sounder basis than it had been formerly.

At the same time, Morris's name came to be indelibly linked to the site for other, more personal reasons. With the urging of the American Museum, he erected and occupied a house compatible in its style with that of the ancients in front of the Anasazi structure. Now incorporated into the monument headquarters and visitors' center, its masonry walls were fashioned from fallen building stones originally shaped and laid by the Pueblo Indians. For several years after excavations halted, Morris served as governmental custodian, guiding a growing tide of visitors through the ruins and imparting to them his personal enthusiasm for this bit of the national patrimony. At the request of the National Park Service, he later supervised the restoration of a specialized ceremonial chamber, or Great Kiva, in the village's central plaza that today remains an unusual attraction among Southwestern archaeological features. He donated his well-worn set of tools consisting of whisk broom, paint

brush, dental pick, trowel, and geologist's pick for a permanent display in the monument's small museum. And finally at the end of a long illustrious career, one dawn in 1956 his own ashes were raked into the sandy floor of an inner room within the West Ruin which more than thirty years previously he had helped to uncover.

Once the vegetation was grubbed off the West Ruin preparatory to excavation, its impressive size and configuration were apparent. Morris described the first work at the site as follows.

In July 1916, when the Museum's party arrived at Aztec ready to begin the initial stages of the contemplated explorations, the ruin resembled nothing more than a patch of jungle rising in the midst of cultivated fields. Alfalfa was growing upon the north, south, and east sides, while on the other side of a fence that skirted the western base of the mound stood a young and flourishing apple orchard. The refuse mounds at the southeast and southwest corners, as well as a strip of varying width bordering the alfalfa fields, supported a rank growth of sunflowers and other weeds, in places at least eight feet high. A thicket of chico brush hid the court and the contours of the four structures which surround it, the walls of the central portion of the north wing alone being visible above the tangled vegetation. Trails connected the various openings that gave access to the chambers with intact ceilings which had been burrowed into by relic hunters years previously, but for the most part, the area was impassable except to those clad with sufficiently heavy garments to resist the thorns, or to those resigned to endure the itching torment which results from the slightest abrasion of the skin by the twigs of the chico.

After the brush had been cut, piled, and burned, it was possible to obtain a fairly definite conception of the ruin with a single sweep of the eye. Three long mounds, marking the sites of the east, west, and north wings, enclosed three sides of a rectangular court which was bordered on the south by a low crescentic embankment concealing the remains of an arc-shaped row of rooms. Most of the mounds covering the west wing stood twenty feet high, while the walls of the north wing rose in some places twenty-nine feet above their original foundations. The mound of the east wing varied from five feet in height at its junction with the south wing, to twenty feet at its northern extremity.

The main outline and gross dimensions of the groundplan were apparent before excavations were begun, showing the ruin to have been a structure roughly 359 by 280 feet, built about a court whose approximate dimensions are 180 by 200 feet. (Morris 1919: 10–13)

After intensive, albeit what turned out to be partial, excavation, it was determined that the Anasazi community had consisted of an astounding 353 rooms arranged in a basically rectangular plan around an open central courtyard. These included 221 contiguous interconnected rooms on ground level, a tier of 119 rooms on a second story, and 12 units on a third elevation. Also present were 29 circular ceremonial rooms, or small kivas, presumably used by individual social groups such as clans, constructed within the domestic assemblage or less commonly beneath the surface of the court, and a much larger, isolated, semisubterranean Great Kiva in the plaza intended for use by the entire populace. Quite surely not all rooms were living quarters nor housed contemporary families of equal size, but perhaps over what was then believed to have been a long stretch of time, Morris determined that 700–1,000 people had lived there—a figure considered too high by some archaeologists today. The town arrangement was what today would be considered a viable one receptive to solar benefits. The highest wing was along the colder north elevation but without northward openings other than modest ones for ventilation and light placed just beneath ceiling rafters. The lowest room block was on the south so that winter sunshine could spread its warmth on to the flat roofs and plaza of the complex, where most daily activities are assumed to have taken place. The large size of the structure and the concentration of population within it, encompassing a span of time later determined to have been two centuries, were found to be unusual in the Anasazi Animas valley. They remain unmatched in modern times there because typically the settlement pattern is a limited one of familial dispersal.

As excavation proceeded, it became evident that many features revealed at Aztec aligned it to an already defined major Anasazi core center, that of Chaco Canyon to the south. This relationship could be seen in Aztec's southern orientation and town plan, its large aggregation of cellular rooms in a multilevel communal edifice erected on open terrain and accessible only through a single portal, its style of masonry featuring the employment of tabular sandstone blocks, the presence of both clan and Great Kivas, and its idiosyncracies of room size, ceiling height, and door shape and dimensions. At Chaco, over a dozen similar large ruins were known to represent a comparable peak of the San Juan Anasazi.

As more of the Aztec Ruins was cleared of dirt, it was learned that the history of the erection and use of the pueblo had not been as simple as first supposed. Not only had there been frequent remodeling by the first builders, but the architectural evolution of the place had been compounded by alien elements which could only have been those related to the Mesa Verde expression of the Anasazi. It became evident that Aztec Ruins had been neither solely Chacoan nor a hybridization of two contemporaneous overlapping cultural interpretations of the Anasazi, one from the south and one from the northwest. The arrangement of cultural deposits in stratigraphic positions made it clear that what had occurred there during a time that was being recognized as a zenith period of Anasazi development had been two distinct successive occupations by

provincials removed from their particular heartlands and perhaps separated from each other by a long period of time. Furthermore, there was the nagging suspicion that others had lived and farmed on this same terrace before them.

As Morris came to conceptualize the sequence of aboriginal events, the original town had been erected by people either directly from Chaco Canyon or greatly influenced by developments already adopted there. Perhaps these first residents had moved no farther than from numerous smaller villages of Chaco affiliation known to have been established already along the San Juan drainage. Apparently, at some era in their history, economic or defensive needs drew these Anasazi together into a large social agglomeration. Morris interpreted their stay at the west pueblo at Aztec as having been lengthy because of the three feet or more of trash which had drifted across surrounding fields and three seven-foot high heaps of cast-off occupational debris. Then these folks once again gradually moved on. The Chacoan communal great house stood empty and untended for years. A fine layer of sand and adobe filtered through its ceilings and unsealed doorways to lay a thin sterile blanket within its lifeless quarters.

Still in reclaimable condition, subsequently the structure was partially reoccupied by other, perhaps more numerous, Anasazi migrants bearing variants of material traits more characteristic of the Mesa Verdians. Why they came was unknown, and so was their precise former home. However, along the La Plata drainage a short distance to the west Morris had observed a comparable reoccupation sequence. These incidents of successive utilization of villages suggested that instead of one exodus from the northern San Juan, as had been thought, there actually had been two. The first was by the Chacoans, the later by those from the Mesa Verde area.

While the Mesa Verdians erected houses of their own on the same river terrace, they also moved into several old Chacoan towns such as Aztec, cleared out or built over discarded debris left behind by former tenants, and proceeded to change them according to their own tastes. Taking a clue from the possessions thrown away, the western room block at Aztec appeared to have been their preferred part of the original pueblo. The Mesa Verdians made some rooms smaller through erection of partitions. They lowered ceilings, often by reusing timbers yanked from fallen sections of the structure. They changed shape and size of passage openings, closed up unneeded apertures, built interior bins and platforms, added kivas like those to which they were accustomed or modified the Chacoan ones, and tacked on rooms across the south and out to the west side of the compound in what Morris called the Annex. For most of this new construction at Aztec and dozens of other small villages in the vicinity, the Mesa Verdians used easily obtainable cobblestones rather than going to the trouble of shaping hard sandstone. They also built some adobe walls reinforced by horizontal poles set into their cores. When they used sandstone masonry, it lacked the quality of that of the Chacoans, being more irregular and carelessly set.

After dwelling in the pueblo for some decades, the Mesa Verdians suffered a disastrous upheaval which caused them to pack up a few belongings and walk away from the Animas valley forever. According to Morris, this departure may have been precipitated by raiders who set fire to the village, or maybe the residents themselves burned their emptied town. In either case, it is puzzling why the western wing was spared. As evidenced in the eastern and northern arms of the building from lenses of charcoal and charred beams, the fires may be more plausibly explained as domestic tragedies resulting from hearth flames out of control rather than any purposeful action by the tenants or their hypothetical enemies.

When the West Ruin was cleared, it was seen that the ruin consisted of four units of differing heights around an open central courtyard. In 1916 the main problem was one of mapping out a plan for attacking the huge piles of exposed debris. Just the volume of the overburden to be removed was intimidating. Courtesy University of Colorado Museum.

Morris first proposed to erect some kind of sluice box with water from a neighboring irrigation ditch to flush away the excavated dirt, leaving heavier cultural objects in the grooves. That plan fortunately was scrapped because of the possibility of small objects being swept away by the water's action and for fear that other items might suffer damage from moisture. Horses and scrapers, being the earth removal equipment of the day, were chosen for the initial season's clearing. The overburden was dug up by picks and shovels, carefully examined for artifacts, and moved by scrapers to central locations where it was then put into ore cars pulled by horses over tracks to dump locations adjacent to the ruins.

Work was begun at the southeastern corner of the compound, working northward along the eastern wing. The unit proved to be unlike the exposed walls in the north wing. Uncovered were cellular rooms constructed of cobblestones embedded in large quantities of mud mortar. As the excavators steadily progressed north, the walls, however, changed to the sandstone block masonry typical of the standing walls of the north wing.

By the end of the 1916 season, 34 rooms and 3 kivas had been opened up. Some masonry walls had been repaired, and one kiva in the courtyard had been reroofed. Courtesy University of Colorado Museum.

Dirt from the excavated rooms was shoveled up on to wooden ground-level platforms where it was screened in order to reclaim small artifacts. An ore cart and a section of narrow gauge track, such as were used in mines, can be seen in this photo. They were employed to haul the spoil dirt to dumps adjacent to the ruins. Some of the dirt was used to build dikes to protect fields or to construct sections of road foundations. Courtesy University of Colorado Museum.

The best preserved of the clan kivas excavated in 1916, designated Kiva E, had been sunk into the central courtyard near to the east wing. It was a partially subterranean circular chamber first constructed by the Chacoan settlers but it had been substantially remodeled by later Mesa Verdians. Its clearing was difficult because of the looseness of the surrounding dirt and rocks that continually sluffed off into the opened pit. This is a view of it looking west, the Animas River in the upper left background having made its westward turn toward the San Juan. Courtesy University of Colorado Museum.

Kiva E was rebuilt and reroofed in 1916.

The view above shows clearing and restoration work in progress simultaneously, the partly cleared east wing in the background. Courtesy University of Colorado Museum.

To the left is a portion of the completed interior as interpreted by Morris. Later research, however, showed that some of the details were incorrectly reconstructed. The central firepit most probably had been at floor level without connecting walls to the southern recess. The presence of two benches, one at sitting level and another higher one to support the pilasters, was open to question.

The cribbed roof of peeled juniper logs was copied after one in a cliff dwelling in Mesa Verde National Park. These logs, based upon the pilasters, were covered with a layer of juniper splits and an upper flat capping of earth that probably stood a foot or so above the courtyard surface. Entrance was through a rooftop hatchway. (The ladder at the upper left is a modern type used for the convenience and safety of visitors rather than an aboriginal model with slender rungs.) Courtesy National Park Service.

A temporary work shed was erected in the plaza adjacent to the east wing in the background of this view. For a while it not only provided storage for tools and supplies, it served as a bunkhouse for Morris and a place to display the recovered specimens.

In the right center is Kiva E after it had been excavated and reroofed. Below that, a smaller kiva is being excavated with the aid of a hoist and bucket. Dirt from that excavation is being screened for small specimens. At the lower left are cement capped tops of masonry walls of the north wing. Courtesy University of Colorado Museum.

The partially intact cribbed log roof of a kiva in Square Tower House, Mesa Verde National Park, was studied by Morris to ascertain how it was built so that similar construction methods could be followed in reroofing Kiva E at Aztec, attributed to Mesa Verdians. The photo shows the cribbed logs resting upon pilasters, the layer of juniper splints, and the uppermost covering of dirt. Courtesy University of Colorado Museum.

At the end of the opening season, the mounds of the West Ruin were being dissected to reveal a well defined rectangular structure of contiguous rooms. This view, taken in the fall, shows the partly excavated one-story arc of crudely built cobblestone rooms across the southern limits of the site, the central masonry-walled rooms of the cleared east wing and the later accretion of less substantial units on the southeast corner, and the roof of reconstructed Kiva E. The northeast end of the north wing had been partly cleared and some walls had been repaired. The rubble in the center foreground resulted from the excavations and was stockpiled for use in restoration of masonry walls. Courtesy University of Colorado Museum.

The villagers were fascinated by the activities taking place in their hometown ruin, and they came to observe in steadily increasing numbers. Morris reported to the museum that several dozen onlookers a day was not uncommon and that one day over a hundred curious persons had put in an appearance. A local newspaper reported about 1917 that the ruins were becoming a popular place to visit and that Mr. Morris was a most courteous and painstaking guide, who presented details about the excavations and restoration in a competent and pleasing manner.

Such a ringside audience was undoubtedly distracting at times to the workers and their director, but it was the beginning of a vital partnership between scientific and non-scientific sectors of the society. The interest that came through observation and understanding would make it easier for taxpayers to accept their assessments for maintenance of significant archaeological sites, such as Aztec Ruins, that came to be held in permanent trust for the public by the federal government. Courtesy University of Colorado Museum.

The first season proved the mine trams and their flimsy rails inadequate for the weight and volume of overburden that had to be carried off the site. They were discarded and broad-bedded farm wagons pulled by teams of horses or mules were substituted.

Workers were paid $2.50 a day, $4 if they supplied a team of animals. After a strike, wages raised to $3. This figure was protested by other employers of the region as being inflationary. Moreover, after World War I broke out, it was charged that labor was being taken by the excavations that was needed elsewhere. To pacify the protestors, the museum issued orders that whenever there were farm needs that called for attention, all hands were to halt work at the ruins and tend to the more pressing affairs.

Nevertheless, by the end of 1918 Morris was able to report to the American Museum of National History that 137 rooms had been cleared and that 6,500 cubic yards of dirt and rubble had been removed. With satisfaction, he wrote, "The importance of the exploration of the Aztec Ruin is three-fold: first, because of the scientific data which it yields; second, because of the pleasing and instructive exhibits which it furnishes for the halls of the Museum; and third, because for the world at large it is providing *in situ* a permanent and attractive monument to the arts and material accomplishments of the aborigines of the Southwest, which will prove, as the years pass, to be of constantly increasing educational value." Courtesy University of Colorado Museum.

A visitor crouches in a doorway of the north wing complex of the second-story rooms. The masonry above and to the left of the opening already had been reset in cement, its color obvious as compared to the untouched surrounding walls. Similar rebuilding of the room to the left is detectable. Courtesy University of Colorado Museum.

Looking down from a height in the north wing, the cleared eastern room block and kivas are highlighted by shadows. The tops of the walls have been capped with cement to help preserve them. To the left and in the foreground, workers are shoveling sterile dirt into waiting wagons. In the center, piles of rocks and sand await use in rebuilding and repairing fallen or weakened walls. Morris's truck is parked in the plaza at the right. Courtesy University of Colorado Museum.

Stabilization work in the east wing involved pointing the uppermost course with cement or pouring a cement capping on top of the wall. Aboriginally the interiors of all these masonry walls were covered with mud plaster. A second-story level with several doorways can be observed on the left. Although no original roofs remained, these particular rooms were among the most productive in terms of artifact yield, especially those of vegetal substance. Some rooms were filled with more than ten feet of such refuse beneath fallen timbers, wall elements, and drifted dirt. In addition to the fiber specimens, there was a great variety and amount of objects of bone, stone, leather, and earthenware.

The circular unit to left center is a small clan kiva of Mesa Verde–style incorporated into the house mass after it was reoccupied in the thirteenth century. Access to it would have been through a hatchway in the floor of a second story room above. The corner spaces between the circular chamber and the surrounding rectangular walls had been filled by its builders with sand or small gravel. The cluster of highest walls to the upper left is the center of the north wing. The photograph was taken in 1917 or 1918.

At lower right a 1940 view of the same ▷ room block shows repair of the walls of a Chaco style kiva nearing completion by a National Park Service stabilization crew. Lined up against the base of some east wing rooms are a number of metates, or grinding slabs, from the excavations.

Note that the earlier method of capping walls with cement, as can be seen on walls in the background, has been replaced by a more efficient and less detractive technique in which several upper courses are reset in tinted cement, soil cement, or mud mortar.

Photos courtesy University of Colorado Museum.

Excavation was increasingly laborious as diggers' shovels, picks, and mattocks ate their way down through several collapsed stories of debris. The bottom floor of some room shafts was thirty feet below the surrounding ruin surface. Removing the fill from that depth meant shoveling the dirt up several successive platforms until it reached the surface and could be taken to an open space for screening. This step was imperative so that small items, especially potsherds, would not be overlooked and to record the proper origin of all specimens. Courtesy University of Colorado Museum.

Room 41 of the east wing had been the scene of a conflagration destroying the ceiling between the two stories, allowing over 200 bushels of charred corn still on the cob to fall from the upper room where it had been stored to the room below. Present also were a number of burials that had been disturbed by falling walls or rats.

More than 31,000 small, black, disc-shaped stone beads, which when restrung made a strand 75-feet long, were picked from the room fill by exacting search that included use of a fine mesh screen, then an even finer milk sieve, and finally a magnifying glass. Morris, with his back to the camera, worked alongside crew members to ensure total recovery. At the right center a large jar and a pair of deer antlers await removal. Courtesy University of Colorado Museum.

One of the local farmers who worked for Morris at the Aztec Ruins and later on other expeditions was Oley Owens. He is shown standing before a block of compacted debris rich with vegetal materials within a dry room. Although he had mini-mal formal education, Owens proved to be a skilled, practical field man with a keen interest in archaeology and frequently served as caretaker of the ruins during Morris's absences. Courtesy University of Colorado Museum.

One dry interior storage room produced about a cord of cottonwood bark and slabs. Morris judged it had been stripped from green trees by some flat-pointed instrument that had been inserted and driven beneath the bark and wood. The intended purpose of this material is unknown. Courtesy University of Colorado Museum.

While excavation work was in progress, the ruin remained unfenced. Dawn often saw animals from neighboring farms wandering about the site. With the new cement capping on wall tops, their hoofs were not apt to loosen the rocks. Courtesy University of Colorado Museum.

Archaeology can be dirty work, even for 28-year-old project director Earl Morris, who is shown standing in front of the work shed in the plaza of the ruin about 1917. Courtesy University of Colorado Museum.

Excavation and repair of the two-storied
north wing consumed much of the 1917
and 1918 field seasons. Before lower levels could be cleared, it was imperative for
the preservation of the building and the
safety of those working around it to reset
unstable walls. From the north the large
sections of repaired walls are visible
above rectangular doorways in two
rooms. Workers are busy at a mortar box
and on a makeshift scaffold. Courtesy
University of Colorado Museum.

Repair of the exterior or north face of the north wing was a major undertaking, because most of the remaining original facing had to be removed and reset in cement. Both of these photographs, taken during that job, clearly reveal the core-and-veneer style of masonry construction employed by the twelfth-century Chacoans who were the original builders of the west pueblo. Wall hearts consisted of irregular stones bedded in mud. Each face of the wall was then covered with neatly laid rows of shaped stones. These views show work along the outer wall of the building at the juncture between the first and second stories. The square openings with pole lintels were ventilation passages usually set just below the room's ceiling. The stub end of two large primary beams, 700 years old, can be seen projecting through the wall core of the top of a first story room.

Photos courtesy University of Colorado Museum.

ARCHITECTURE

The predominant architecture of the West Ruin was one of multiple, flat roofed, rectangular units of sandstone masonry set side by side in contiguous rows. The north wing was composed of five and six rows of rooms from south to north, with more second-story units than occurred elsewhere. The east wing had five room rows from plaza to outer wall, the uncleared west wing was seven rows deep, and the aberrant, slightly bowed south wing was merely one row. As the walls were laid, the rubble cores were hidden by a surface finish on each face of shaped sandstone blocks set up neatly in courses that alternated in bulk and sometimes in color to create aesthetically pleasing contrasts of scale and hue. The variations between rows of thick blocks and thinner chinking gave rise to its being known now as banded masonry. One striking band along the exterior of the western flank and in several interior rooms was made of green stones obtained from a source not yet located by researchers. The carefully executed veneer was unbonded to the core, thereby creating a structural weakness to be exploited later by destructive forces. Both its beauties and its defects were concealed under a thick layer of mud plaster whose color and softened contours had made the exterior building mass appear an integral part of the landform out of which it grew. The masonry was not as finely done as that at Chaco Canyon because the locally available sandstone did not fracture in the same kinds of straight cleavage planes. Interiors of rooms also were plastered. Usually this coating was uncolored clay tempered with sand, but examples were found of red tinted wainscoting contrasted with gypsum white upper walls and some incised or painted patterns. One especially fine room also was decorated with white hand prints on ceiling beams. Several grinding slabs were recovered upon which deep red stains from pulverizing iron oxide suggests their former use in preparation of the colored wall wash. By the time of excavation, the outside mud layers had melted away, leaving the masonry exteriors as naked as when they were first erected. Even though some inside plaster remained, frequently blackened by the smoke of cook fires, it was considered a pity that more had not survived because rows of red and white rooms surely had lifted the spirits of the inhabitants. Despite their overall excellence, other engineering weaknesses of walls, such as unbonded corners and absence of offset coursing, were in evidence.

In the lack of documentation or remains of scaffolding, one can only speculate about the way in which such masonry walls on the unbroken exterior face of the pueblo could have been raised sheer for two or more stories. Probably it was a matter of many human backs carrying baskets of mud mortar and shaped stones up ladders to higher levels in the interior of the building and masons leaning over raised wall cores from temporary platforms, stringers, piles of construction debris, and roofs already in place to put final outer materials into position. Another possible aid in reaching upper exterior surfaces was what may have been a balcony along the north wall. The evidence for it was inconclusive, but such adjuncts were known in sites at Chaco Canyon and Mesa Verde. Morris postulated that the eastern wing had been constructed in two principal increments, with some later accretions on its southern limits. There also seemed to have been an earlier cobblestone construction beneath parts of this arm of the compound, but it remained unexplored. The north wing apparently had been raised in one preplanned master effort. Definite information about the Chaco stages of building in the west wing await future clearing. Parts of it also may have been erected over some dismantled houses of unknown age. The south wing that closed off the plaza, consisting of cobblestone and adobe units, was viewed as part of the later Mesa Verde revitalization of the town.

Nineteen of the original room ceilings remain in place, making Aztec Ruins a remarkable display of Anasazi architectural expertise. The ceilings were elaborate assemblages of pine or juniper supporting beams of large diameters that spanned the narrow dimensions of rooms, over which closely spaced pine, juniper, or cottonwood poles were placed in the opposite direction. These poles sometimes were topped by a willow matting held together with yucca lashing whose main purpose, other than being decorative, was to curtail a shower of dust particles from above. Universally above them was a layer of juniper splints covered with a thick deposit of tamped earth that formed either an exposed roof or the floor of an upper room.

Concentrated in the southeast corner of the pueblo and in the eastern half of the north wing and adjacent plaza were a number of kivas. They all were oriented on a north-south axis. As the archaeologists later reconstructed the history of this architectural form, it had its roots in an ancestral pithouse. At the beginning of their cultural continuum, the pithouse had been a place where activities relevant to both religious and secular Anasazi life had been carried out. When the Anasazi decided to build surface storage units and shelters, they retained the subterranean chamber as a sacred place, adding some features to it that through time became highly standardized. The kiva was almost always circular, though the original pithouses had seldom been so uniformly shaped. If it was not actually below ground level, the kiva was incorporated into a complex of rooms in such a way as to make it appear so. To emphasize this subterranean character, entrance to the kiva was through a roof hatchway that also served as a smoke hole. Interiors were equipped with a bench around the lower wall upon which pilasters were placed to support a vaulted cribbed roof of beams topped with splints and earth. Here were two elements that distinguished sacred from profane Anasazi constructions. If the bench was meant for seating of participants in the kiva ceremonies, that was a novel comfort because ordinary houses lacked any such facilities, and flat roofs were universal for all structures other than kivas. In the center of the kiva floor was a firepit directly beneath the hatchway—smoke hole. Aligned to the north of most Anasazi kivas was a small symbolic hole to the underground spirit world, the sipapu. Also called the earth-navel, it is the mythical place of emergence of the people from their place of physical and cultural development within the earth. The sipapu further denotes the point of contact between the natural world and the supernatural underworld where the spirit people, the kachinas, live and to where the dead return. To the south, a low upright stone slab or masonry wall protected the hearth from air currents flowing out of a ventilator shaft opening to the outside.

At the Aztec West Ruin the original kivas were faced with the same style masonry as the houses. Where they had been incorporated into the rectangular building units, the corner spaces between the curvature of their walls and the adjacent straight room walls had been filled with clean sand that obviously had been scooped up nearby because it usually contained bits of pottery and charcoal. This elimination of surrounding exterior space was the builders' way of making these particular chambers more structurally secure and to appear subterranean. The smoke from their hearths surely wafted through the second story. Most Aztec kivas of this primary occupancy lack sipapus, which is an attribute of contemporaneous Chaco kivas.

The characteristic Mesa Verde kiva style called for a small recess of unknown purpose in the southern wall, giving the structure a keyhole shape. The ventilator shaft exited beneath this recess. At Aztec when persons influenced by the northern San Juan Anasazi conventions built or remodeled kivas, they put in this recess and frequently resorted to cobblestones rather than sandstone blocks for lining the entire pit. Most of their kivas were located in the southwestern part of the compound and nearby Annex. However, during the first season of excavation at the West Ruin, a large remodeled cobblestone-lined kiva (Kiva E) was found in the open court near the east wing. It was repaired and reroofed temporarily so that visitors could gain a better idea of how such a chamber would have appeared when functioning.

In the house blocks doorways were rectangular or T-shaped, the latter theorized to have been accommodation for a person carrying a shoulder or head burden. A few doorways were put in room corners. The use of such a critical juncture showed either daring or considerable engineering skill, and the fact that many never collapsed underscores the latter. The door openings were a foot or so above the floor level and were no more than several feet wide and three or four feet high. They reduced drafts which could have been troublesome for cooking or heating fires in floor-level hearths. When no longer needed, the door openings were sealed with the same kind of coursed masonry as the surrounding walls. When their size was considered unnecessarily great, they were partly plugged with plastered-in portions of willow matting. Many rooms were connected in at least one direction by such openings, but some had doors on two,

three, or all four walls. Openings out of the room maze were into the enclosed central court. Doorway closures were rare. Matting, skins, textiles, or stone slabs could have been used.

Several unique passageways ran diagonally from the upper corner wall of a first-floor room into a second-story chamber, so giving access between levels. However, three extant first-floor ceiling hatchways and several recovered runged ladders indicate that their use was the more typical means of getting into upper stories.

Windows were non-existent. Some rooms were equipped with air conditioning in the form of foot square openings in outer walls or ventilator shafts that ran beneath floors of adjoining rooms until an exterior opening was reached. Nevertheless, sufficient fresh air in innermost rooms must have been a problem.

For storage purposes some bins were created in room corners by upright stone slabs, niches were left in wall faces, and occasionally large earthenware jars were sunk below floors with their mouths at ground level covered by stone lids. Diggers learned to detect them by the hollow sound they produced when shovels struck the floor. Otherwise there were only rare built-in pegs, platforms, or shelves for hanging or piling objects. Certainly some units within the more central portions of the house blocks had always been intended for storage rather than for eating and sleeping purposes. Morris noted that a number of such

Nineteen original ceilings remain in first-floor rooms of the West Ruin and thirteen others are known to exist in the closed East Ruin. Their preservation can be attributed to the expertise of the builders which prevented collapse, a sealing deposit of cultural and natural materials above the roof that curtailed leakage but did not cause undue pressure, an arid environment, and escape from destructive fires and equally destructive vandals. This photograph looks up from floor level to part of a smoke-and-age-darkened ceiling about 10 feet above.

Four construction elements can be seen. Several large stringers, such as the one shown, were set across the narrow dimension of the room. On top of the stringers running in the opposite direction, were small, straight, peeled poles. Rush matting or a layer of juniper splints, as in this example, topped the secondary poles. Finally, a heavy deposit of mud was tamped over the matting or splints to form the outer roof in single-story units or the floor of upper-occupational levels.

Some seepage has occurred in this room but not enough to peel a layer of mud plaster from the walls. A ventilation opening appears in the lower right in a customary position just below the ceiling. Courtesy National Park Service.

rooms lacked hearths and their floors were unstained from spillage and foot traffic. Other better ventilated rooms had one or more small circular firepits edged with stones in their corners or centers, confirm-ing their domiciliary usage. A few rooms contained grinding bins outlined by stone slabs. In several instances a milling slab or metate was still in place within them.

Looking down from a high position in a second-story room, the composition of the ceiling-floor divider between levels is well illustrated. At the right a section of the earthen floor remains. A stone-lined grinding bin appears on it with a metate still in place. To the left of the floor appears the juniper splint covering beneath which is a layer of small parallel poles arranged along the long axis of the room. They are supported by paired beams across the narrow axis. Below is the darkness of the first-floor room. Two small wall niches for storage can be seen on the right wall. Courtesy University of Colorado Museum.

Another less well preserved second-story room contained evidence for identical ceiling construction, with beams, topped by poles, and then splints in alternating direction. The dirt floor of the second level had sifted down into the room below. The walls depicted reveal a modified banded type of masonry still lightly coated with a film of mud plaster. Courtesy University of Colorado Museum.

In some rooms rush matting bound with yucca cordage had been placed between ceiling poles and the upper bed of juniper splints or earthen layer. Although the mats were decorative when seen from below, their principal purpose most probably was to inhibit the downward filtering of dirt and dust from the earth floor or roof above. This practice would have been appreciated by Spanish colonial settlers in the Southwest, who, upon adopting Pueblo Indian architecture, found it necessary to drape textiles beneath their ceilings for the same reason. Courtesy University of Colorado Museum.

When the first settlers in the Animas valley broke their way into the northern room block of the West Ruin through jagged holes they made in the walls such as on the right, they encountered rooms comparable to the one pictured here. Standing walls often had been stripped by time and moisture of their plaster coatings. Many of the ceilings remained at least partly intact. Usually one or more narrow open doors situated above floor level connected to adjoining rooms. In some instances a drift of refuse had poured in through breaks in the roofs above, leaving cracked timbers poking out at sharp angles. Often such abandoned habitations had served as burial sites for the dead. The individual lying on the room floor at the lower right had been flexed into the customary burial position and covered with a piece of matting. Nearby pottery bowls and a mug had been left as funerary offerings. In this case and the majority of others encountered during excavation, the ceramics were those of the Mesa Verde tradition. Courtesy University of Colorado Museum.

Doorways were sometimes closed by "Venetian blind-like" willow twig or rush mats such as seen here. In this case, however, it appears as though someone wanted to make the opening smaller and, after erecting a framework of small poles, placed the mat in the upper part of the aperture and covered it and the poles, as we do lath, with mud plaster. Large stone slabs and skins also were used to close doorways. Set up on the sill of the doorway by the photographer are some stone axes and manos (hand-propelled rectangular stones that were used on metates in the grinding of vegetal materials such as corn). Courtesy National Park Service.

Most interior room walls had been coated with untinted mud plaster. A few more elaborate rooms, such as this second-story one in the north wing, were decorated with a low brick red band above which was an expanse of gypsum whitewash. Further decoration here consisted of sets of red triangles inserted into the white zone. Morris considered this room, which also had an intact ceiling, to have been of twelfth-century Chacoan construction subsequently remodeled in the thirteenth century by Mesa Verdians. Courtesy University of Colorado Museum.

Corner or diagonal doorways, providing access diagonally from one room to another, are a rare item in the Anasazi architectural school, but when found, they tend to cluster predominately in Chaco Canyon or within the realm of Chaco influence. Several examples, such as this, can be seen in the West Ruin. Considerable engineering skill and prudent architectural planning are demonstrated in putting a doorway between the corners of two rooms. Courtesy National Park Service.

Two or more distinct stories usually are easy to recognize in room shafts where the separating roof structure has disappeared. In this photograph, the end of a supporting beam remains above the lower rectangular doorway. The irregular section of masonry above it represents the old ceiling-floor level. A good idea can be gained of how high the narrow second-floor door was above the floor (elevations and restricted openings such as these were energy efficient). Note that the wall on the left abuts against the one on the right and that no sign of bonding to tie the walls together is in evidence. Courtesy National Park Service.

ARTIFACTS

At present the pristine condition of the rooms readied for visitation gives no hint of the conditions that prevailed when the house was alive with Anasazi men, women, and children. Once the overburden of fallen timbers and rocks was skinned from it, the excavators of the West Ruin discovered that, particularly during the Mesa Verdian tenancy, the structure had functioned not only as shelter for the living but as a giant mausoleum and an incredible city dump and toilet. Random abandoned chambers had been convenient places in which to deposit bodies; 186 bodies and stray bones of others which had been scattered by rats had been found before work ceased. Some had been nestled in shallow pits in the earthen floors, but others had been left on the exposed floor surfaces or in a cushioning pile of trash to be drifted over by additional dumping. Elsewhere room after room had been jammed to the ten-foot-high ceilings with the accumulated residues of human existence. These ranged from worn out or broken articles to others that for unfathomable reasons had been cast aside while still serviceable, from stocks of foodstuffs and raw resources for various tools and utensils to masses of excrement. One dog appeared to have been sealed in a room and left to die of starvation, his frantic clawing on a plastered wall still clearly visible.

The stench from these deposits, the inevitable swarms of bugs and rodents attracted to them, the unsanitary discomforts of close living in dimly lit rooms stifling with human smells and the smoke of open fires, and the dampness trapped by heavy stone walls surely made West Ruin no paradise on the Animas. Probably conditions were no more uncomfortable than in many other Anasazi settlements, but at Aztec the arid climate, massive walls, and durable ceilings foster such an amazing degree of preservation that a shocking picture of life as it was is more vividly imparted.

Getting at the burials and artifacts important for anthropological interpretation was complicated by the relentless deterioration of the abandoned dwelling. Water from rains and melted snow had pooled on dirt roofs and slowly rotted or split the heavy wooden elements beneath, which then crashed down from their heights. In their fall they loosened or carried chunks of wall with them. Where wall cores had been exposed, they absorbed moisture that under conditions of freezing and thawing caused the veneer facing to buckle and peel off. Some lower rooms were entirely choked with tons of rubble from the earthward descent of several stories. In units consumed by fires, the remaining debris that frequently had poured from upper floor levels into lower chambers was larded with charcoal that blackened diggers head to toe. Many double-storied rooms, where intervening ceilings had been destroyed, were shafts up to thirty feet deep. This necessitated fill dirt to be shoveled upward on to platforms at successively higher elevations or be hoisted up in wooden boxes, finally to be carefully screened before being hauled away from the ruin. When hardened debris that had filled some units like concrete was removed, the sounds of crashing rocks and splintering beams sent diggers scurrying for open ground. Underlying cultural deposits in demolished rooms, often frosted with thick accumulations of generations of rat nests, dung, and carcasses, and what Morris described as "yards of desiccated bull snakes," clouded with dust and unpleasant odors when disturbed. Other exposed layers of vegetable matter had decomposed into a disagreeable slime. Yet, perhaps not to the hired hands but definitely to Morris, there were rewards to compensate for such trying excavation.

Amid layers of household sweepings and hearth ash, the enormous variety and volume of specimens recovered comprise a full inventory of the goods the ingenuity of a simple agricultural people had devised from local and sometimes rare natural resources, obtained through trade with their neighbors, for their customary round of everyday activities. With the exception of ceramics made distinctive by certain decorative modes and pigments, whether those folks had been of Chacoan or Mesa Verdian leanings generally could not be determined by their abandoned possessions.

Hammers, adzes, knives, special skinning blades called *tcamahias*, pipes, grinding slabs and handstones, mortars, pestles, pot covers, blades, spear and arrow points, dressed slabs, arrow straighteners, and sandal lasts were made of stone. Bone manufactures were awls, scrapers, spatulas, drills, needles, and ornaments such as beads, rings, and pendants. Thousands of shell beads and many bracelets cut from large mollusks were present, as were fragments of turquoise, abalone shell, and lignite that had been used for jewelry enrichment. One restrung stone necklace of alternating black and white strands reached twelve feet in length.

Several hundred examples of pottery were recovered unbroken. Others were restorable, often shattered by falling debris after being discarded or crushed by the sheer weight of materials dumped on them. Expectedly, because breakage rate was so excessive, potsherds litter all Anasazi sites. They were most abundant at Aztec in otherwise empty rooms, in trash deposits, over the plaza surface and the ground outside the village walls, and even incorporated in mud mortar. Types included utilitarian cooking wares, either plain gray or with roughened exterior surfaces, sooted from long service over fires or as clean as new. Some of these Morris called "archaic," which now causes modern scholars to further suspect an earlier occupation of the environs. Earthenwares slipped white and decorated with black surehanded geometric designs included several variations of bowls, short necked pitchers, bulbous water jars with low-slung horizontal handles, single-handled mugs, dippers with gracefully curved tubular handles that occasionally contained clay pellets as rattles, squat jars with incurved orifices and lids with tiny knobs, miniatures of bowls and other forms, and some vessel fragments that had been reshaped to make what must have been round gaming pieces rather like poker chips.

Most of the ceramics were of the distinctive Mesa Verde vogue. These had relatively thick, highly polished walls whose heavy broadlined ornamentation was carried by a pigment derived from concentrated plant juices. There were some recognizable Chaco-style ceramics bearing a typical patterning based upon thin-lined hatchure played off against solid triangles that was executed in a flat mineral oxide. Some effigies and one rare jar lacquered with a yellow, red, and black pattern also were considered of Chaco influenced derivation. Whether they had been produced locally or at a more central Chaco source was open to debate. The probable reasons that more Chaco pottery did not turn up in the cleared rooms, some of which were found to have as much as five feet of Chaco refuse buried beneath the most recent floor, was that in the Chaco period there also had been three separate trash depositories outside the walls. These likely consumed the bulk of the discarded Chaco earthenwares; however, the extramural dumps were tested only by exploratory trenching. A sample of red wares and some deviant black-on-whites confirmed commercial exchange in ceramics with more southerly contemporaries.

The unusually rich haul of perishable items consisted of wooden arrow shafts, bows, fire drills, snowshoe frames, cylinders of unknown purpose, cradleboards, ladders, knife handles, what were believed to have been altar furnishings, and digging sticks. There were willow and rush mats, fiber or grass pot rests, baskets, fiber hair brushes, yucca rings, cotton cloth headbands or fragments of garments, feather cloth, cordage, tanned hide, moccasins, hoof rattles, single walnut shell beads or groups strung on leather thongs, skin bags, twined or plaited yucca sandals and others made of cloth, gourd bottles, and reed-stemmed cigarettes.

Vegetal remains with importance to the villagers were stashes of corn stalks, tassels, husks, cobs, and kernels. Although tinder dry, they remained green enough to entice nibbling by the expedition's mules. Beans and withered pumpkin rinds indicated use of other vegetables. Representing remains of likely meat supplies were bones of deer, mountain sheep, coyotes, water fowl, beavers, and turkeys. As the only domesticated animal other than dogs, the latter apparently had been penned in one room that also contained ten human bodies. Packs of herbs may have awaited medicinal

demands. Strips of yucca fiber, feathers, quills, and bundles of grass were on hand for various handicrafts. Stored building materials were sheaves of juniper splints, mounds of cottonwood bark and slabs, piles of worked stone, peeled juniper and cottonwood ceiling poles, and stacked willow mats. White gypsum and clay found deposited in one unit may have been intended for plaster, though their use in pottery making cannot be discounted.

The yield of artifacts such as these from any site never approximates the quantity of those articles actually created and used by the ancients. It merely represents a sample or limited cross section but one which, handled judiciously, provides a reasonably reliable platform from which the archaeologist can gain insight into the past.

Perishable artifacts infrequently recovered
from ruins open to the elements were remarkably plentiful in the deep, dry trash
accumulations and in rooms with intact
ceilings in the West Ruin at Aztec. Examples are a plaited basket, above, next to a
pair of deer antlers as found beneath a
burial in a north wing room and a piece
of matting, below, with neatly finished
edges in place in consolidated room fill.
The trash mass around these specimens
contained a great variety of tinder dry vegetal substances.

Photos courtesy University of Colorado
Museum.

Just at quitting time on the day excavations began in a room in the west wing, one of the diggers uncovered an unfamiliar sort of wooden article that was so intriguing that, with the aid of a lantern, Morris worked alone until nearly midnight to unearth it. It turned out to be this six and one-half feet long ladder with four slender rungs (originally it had five) still attached to the two uprights. The ceiling contained one of three hatchways found in rooms of the ruin, leading Morris to the assumption that the ladder had been used to reach the ceiling opening for gaining access to a second-story level. Several other similar ladders were found in the dry deposits of Aztec Ruins. Courtesy National Park Service.

Pottery was everywhere, in the fill, scattered around open ground, and associated with burials. Generally it was broken, but often enough pieces of vessels were found so that they could be reassembled. Hundreds of complete specimens also were recovered, mainly from burials. Morris estimated that ninety percent of the pottery was of Mesa Verdian derivation, as were the examples illustrated in these two views of trash deposits in rooms.

Photos courtesy University of Colorado Museum.

The task of washing the dirt of centuries from batches of potsherds and then sorting them into distinctive categories was a tedious one. It was the only way, however, to ascertain the nature of the finds.

The center pile in the view above contains fragments of white pottery bearing black decorations. The large shattered bowl on top of the heap is Chacoan in appearance. The piles on each side appear to be either undecorated portions of otherwise patterned vessels or fragments of gray cooking pots.

Potsherds from the fill of Room 79 in the north wing from which eight nearly complete vessels were reconstructed line a sorting table below.

At the time of the American Museum of Natural History work at Aztec Ruins, it had not yet become common practice to make exacting tabulations of types of sherds recovered for the purpose of statistical analyses. Nevertheless, Morris had gathered a mass of detailed information about the ceramics retrieved at Aztec, but unfortunately it was never published.

Photos courtesy University of Colorado Museum.

BURIAL PRACTICES

The burials recovered at Aztec West Ruin represent only a small fraction of the number of persons who must have died during the prolonged period of occupation of the great house. They nevertheless had a useful role in site interpretation. Since the San Juan Anasazi were racially identical and culturally compatable, nuances of regional distinctions were determined through details of treatment of the dead on their journeys into the nether world, and, in the case of the West Ruin, the unrelated rubbish that was allowed to literally swallow them. Therefore, because all but a half dozen burials were recovered from overlying trash and they frequently were accompanied by recognizable Mesa Verde pottery, it was believed that many of the interior ground floor rooms of the compound had become a graveyard for those latecomers. Generally one unit contained a single body, but multiple burials per room were not uncommon. Some bodies received respectful attention by being flexed into prenatal positions, covered with feather blankets, cotton cloth, or fiber wrappings, and left with funerary gifts. The fact that they had been placed in littered abandoned houses had no negative significance inasmuch as burial in trash deposits was a time-honored custom among earlier peoples on the Mesa Verde. In this instance, using an enclosing empty house structure was merely a matter of making the most of what was available with the least expenditure of energy. Future archaeological work in Mesa Verde remains would show that during the peak and final period of that regional culture, as that at the Aztec West Ruin, intramural burial was the most typical practice. After excavations closed down, a single case of cremation of five bodies with Mesa Verde style offerings was found in an adjacent field, but this was a highly uncharacteristic burial method for San Juan aborigines.

Still, other burials were obvious minimal efforts. Unwrapped corpses were simply deposited, flexed or extended, out of sight in dark sanctuaries with no comforting cover, no soul satisfying beads, baskets, or pottery bowls. More of these seemingly hastily made burials were in the west wing than in other parts of the town. With one foot in the romantic past of Southwestern archaeology, Morris suggested that inasmuch as many of these deceased were women and children, it could be reasoned that they had been an anguished part of the final desperate band being slowly decimated by disease, disaster, and defeat and their heirs had no wherewithal or remaining desire for appeasement of the gods. It made a heartrending but unsubstantiated scenario.

Despite its being basically a Chaco town, the fact that less than a half dozen identifiable Chaco burials were uncovered in the West Ruin was intriguing but hardly surprising. Few burials other than those of persons with high status had been found during the four-year excavation project at Pueblo Bonito in the 1890s, and a similar dearth was being encountered by National Geographic Society work conducted there simultaneously to that at Aztec. To the archaeologists' consternation, it seemed that the city dwelling Chacoans generally had not liked to put their dead beneath accessible house floors nor in unconsolidated refuse heaps, though the small town dwellers were found to have done so. Where they did dispose of the bulk of them was, and unfortunately has remained, a question.

In the 1920s the Southwest and its richness in archaeological sites and specimens continued to hold great interest for many Easterners. So it was expected that the work under way at Aztec Ruins, sponsored as it was by such a highly regarded institution as the American Museum of Natural History, received an inordinate amount of publicity from East Coast newspapers. Nor was it surprising that the drudgery and grime of excavation in progress and the humble accoutrements of the low level Anasazi were overlooked in favor of a few unusual burials. With limited concrete data yet upon which to rely, little idea of age of remains, and the unfortunate name of the place, frequently misinformation was melodramatic. For example, one skeleton of a man thought to have been over six feet in height and obviously having social prominence because he was accompanied by a coiled basketry shield some three feet in diameter, two knives, two axes, a half dozen bone awls, six pieces of pottery, and two probable digging sticks which the press preferred to regard as swords was introduced via the tabloids to American breakfast tables as "the great warrior of the Aztecs of the village." A young lady of about seventeen years of age, who had suffered a shattered pelvis and forearm, the latter having been splinted, was presented as a flesh-creeping example of primitive osteology. Bluish slag remains of four incinerated children and an adult male, all trapped by a kiva fire, were publicized as evidence of aboriginal mass murder. A male skeleton sprawled within an inside room whose exits had been blocked was said to have been a prisoner condemned to a horrible death. An old woman brutally impaled through the pelvis by a sharpened stake became the "Aztec witch" or an "ill fated American woman of thirty centuries ago." Other more fortunate dead had been laid out with what the papers saw as the family treasures. One such person had gone to his grave with strings of olivella shell beads from throat to thighs while guarding a heap of two hundred quartzite arrowheads and a line of earthenware pots.

Most of the 186 burials exhumed in the West Ruin were within the various house blocks and were individuals deposited in shallow floor pits or merely laid out on the dirt floor. Bodies generally were flexed so that knees and arms were drawn up to the chest. Grave offerings were the rule.

An uncovered burial lies on a room floor. The body appears to have been covered with fiber matting. In the foreground are fragments of other mats.

Left with this flexed individual was an offering of nine complete pottery vessels of assorted shapes and sizes. Some, such as the blackened jar by the head and the corrugated jar at the feet, were obvious utilitarian pots that had seen much usage. The small decorated vessel with a broken horizontal handle is a ladle. It was not uncommon to find several burials in the same room, with later trash strewn over and about them.

Photos courtesy University of Colorado Museum.

Looking down into a room in the west wing, burials can be seen in pits beneath the floor in each of the four corners. Actually the floor was one of three that had covered the room and was smoothed and blackened over its entirety by heavy use. Some time after its abandonment by the Chaco builders, Mesa Verdians took over the room. They remodeled it into a rectangular kiva with central firepit, an ashpit, a deflector, and a floor-level ventilator tunnel that connected with a vertical shaft beyond the south wall. No sipapu was present. Courtesy University of Colorado Museum.

Above is a photographer's arrangement of
the funerary offerings found with a Mesa
Verde burial at Aztec. Items of fiber include matting, cordage, and a woven
band. Of pottery are a mug and three
shallow bowls. A stone metate and several
manos are propped up at the rear. Courtesy National Park Service.

THE GREAT KIVA

Embraced within the courtyard formed by the southern extension of the lateral room blocks was a hugh crater-like depression that was believed to mark the location of a Great Kiva. At least ten such super-sanctuaries already were known in the Chaco Canyon area. A few others had been identified among Mesa Verde remains, though they were regarded as probable intrusive elements from the south. Excavation at Aztec Ruins in the early spring of 1921 proved that indeed there once had been a Great Kiva in active use there and, as in the case of the clan kivas, it was oriented on a north-south axis. Although to that time no other such structure had been thoroughly studied, there were surprises in the Animas example.

For one thing, ringing the gaping hole of the kiva pit proper, whose inside diameter exceeded 41 feet, fourteen unanticipated arc-shaped surface level rooms were found. Each had an exterior doorway that had been sealed at some time, and each was connected to the lower kiva by vertical runged wall slots. The central surface room on the north side was of larger size with special features. It projected rectangularly into the plaza, with an exit opening on the east wall. A stairway from this north alcove and another on the south side, which led to an exit that had been eliminated during prehistoric times, descended to kiva floor level. Kiva and surface walls of sandstone or cobblestone masonry originally had been plastered and painted.

Down on the kiva floor, resurfaced at least nine times with adobe plaster, were the remaining stubs of four masonry pillars nearly three feet square. They had been reinforced as they increased in height by horizontal layers of poles and had been arranged in a square pattern in the center of the structure. They were found to have been footed on a series of four stacked, roughly circular, ponderous slabs of limestone placed at the bottom of a circular hole and bedded on a deep foundation of lignite. Two low masonry benches encircled the entire kiva. However, because no pilasters had been built up from the benches against the masonry wall that lined the kiva, it seemed that rather than the customary cribbed roof of the clan kivas, this Great Kiva and its surface rooms had been covered by one giant circular flat roof that probably had stood ten to twelve feet above the level of the plaza. If so, and taking into consideration the eight-foot depth of the kiva pit, Morris calculated the original height of the four pillar supports to have been about sixteen feet. Reexamination of Chaco Great Kivas confirmed that the same sort of pillar and basal slabs also appeared there. Considering these pillars and remains of fallen roof elements, it was believed that from a central square of beams resting on the pillars at least twenty-three radial beam spokes had stretched around the top of the kiva circumference to form the basic ceiling structure. Over these were lashed layers of smaller saplings and juniper splints such as were used in house ceilings, all then covered with a foot-thick earthen blanket to form the actual roof shell. Morris estimated that, when completed, a roof load of some ninety tons was carried by the fragile wooden framework utilizing no securing nails, tenons, or pegs.

The Great Kivas at Chaco and the one at Aztec contained two three-foot deep masonry vaults which projected eight feet northward across the chamber floor from the base of the two south pillars. These vaults, which were hollow rectangular units perhaps covered by planking in aboriginal times, may have been foot drums, or they may have been places from which concealed medicine men could have appeared suddenly as if by magic during certain rites. A central firepit in direct line with the main north stairs and what might have been an altar in the largest north surface room was found to house a residue of white ash. Other small offering pits were randomly dotted around the remaining floor area.

The Great Kiva at the West Ruin was thought to have served as an intra-community ceremonial building constructed and frequently done over by the founding populace. Judging from its penetration into deposits of accumulated trash, that had occurred well after the initial occupation of the community. It was taken as another line of evidence for some sort of relationship to the classic period Chacoans. Later the edifice was refurbished and used by the Mesa Verdians until such time as its enormous wooden roof caught fire and collapsed. Whether that conflagration coincided with the final abandonment of the pueblo is unknown.

When the Aztec Great Kiva was excavated in February and March of 1921, its floor features and walls, though readily discernible, were in a bad state. This was due to the long exposure following abandonment and poorer workmanship of the final thirteenth-century Mesa Verdian refurbishing efforts. It was felt that without immediate repair the old structure would slump away within a year or two. However, the money needed for such work was not then available, and it would be thirteen years before funds would be appropriated for the rehabilitation of this great sanctuary.

The view here is looking toward the south, the center steps leading up to a surface passageway that opened to the pueblo's courtyard. It adjoined fourteen surface rooms encircling the subterranean chamber. Their access to the kiva floor was by means of vertical slot ladders such as seen in the kiva wall at the upper right. Within the kiva proper the features to be noted are a bench that ran around the entire basal circumference, the bases of two of the four columns that supported the roof and the rectangular floor vaults that extended northward from them, and a fire box in between. The rectangular structure in the center foreground, theorized to have been an altar, was in one of the surface rooms, the northern alcove. Randomly placed holes in the dirt floor can be seen next to the two vaults. Courtesy University of Colorado Museum.

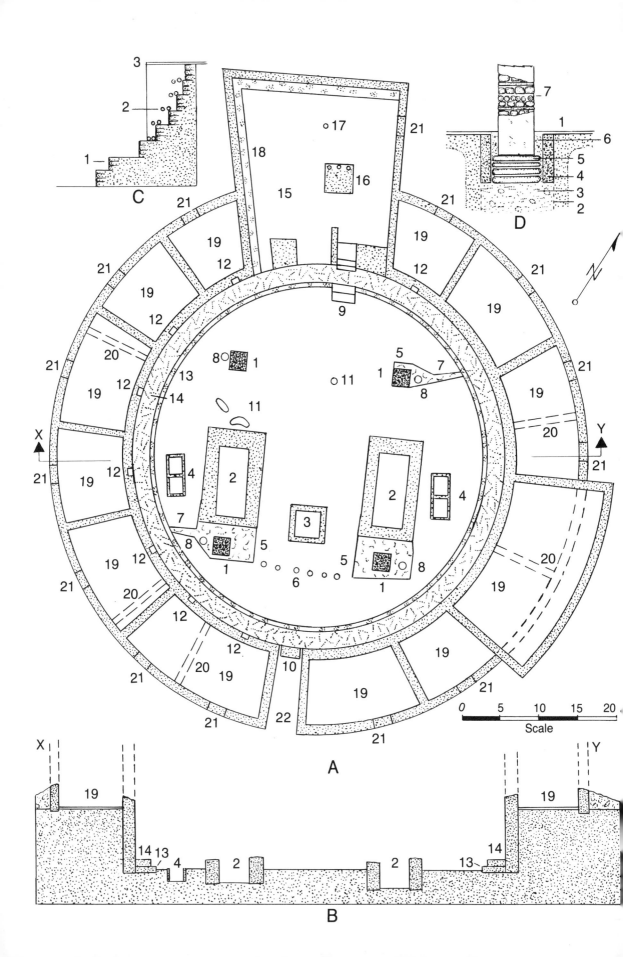

The Aztec Great Kiva.
  A. Plan
  B. Profile
       1. Roof supporting pillars
       2. Vaults
       3. Fire box
       4. Storage boxes
       5. Platform around pillars
       6. Posts of screen or deflector
       7. Walls between pillars and bench
       8. Supplemental timber roof supports
       9. Stairway between kiva and northern alcove
      10. Stairway between kiva and southern passage
      11. Small pits in floor
      12. Slots with ladders between kiva and peripheral rooms
      13. First bench
      14. Later bench
      15. Northern alcove
      16. Altar
      17. Sipapu
      18. Alcove bench
      19. Peripheral surface rooms
      20. Foundations of earlier peripheral rooms
      21. Doorways between peripheral rooms and courtyard
      22. Southern passage
  C. Detail of stairway between kiva and northern alcove
     (Larger scale than A and B)
       1. Masonry steps
       2. Steps of small poles
       3. Alcove floor
  D. Details of roof supporting pillar
     (Larger scale than A and B)
       1. Kiva floor
       2. Pit in kiva floor in which pillar seated
       3. Lignite foundation
       4. Masonry lining of seating pit
       5. Stone discs for supporting pillar
       6. Packed earth
       7. Pillar built of alternating courses of stone masonry and small poles

By 1933 the Great Kiva had melted down to a vestige of its former self. The yearly cycle of thunderstorms and snow had taken its toll, but more troublesome was seepage of ground water from ditches and the irrigating of fields of farms to the north. The Aztec Chamber of Commerce petitioned New Mexico congressmen for immediate action to prevent the structure's total loss.

These three views show that the floor features almost had been eradicated. The surface rooms had melted down and become partially filled with wind- and water-borne sand and dirt.

Kiva E, shown in the upper photo between the Great Kiva and the house block, was repaired and reroofed in 1916. It too was suffering from seepage of ground water.

Photos courtesy National Park Service.

In 1934, with the help of Public Works Administration funds and the services of Earl Morris, loaned to the National Park Service by the Carnegie Institution of Washington by whom he was then employed, the project at the Aztec Great Kiva began. As in the original excavations, the crew was made up of local men, many of whom had known the ruins all their lives and some of whom had helped in its clearing. It had been decided not merely to repair the structure to the state it had been at excavation, no small task in itself, but to completely rebuild it as it would have been when used by the Anasazi. Because such a specialized chamber had never been rebuilt, it was an effort that tested the accuracy of archaeological observation and interpretation and demanded a great deal of practical engineering skill. When the job was done, Morris felt he had definite evidence for every detail of its restoration. The only concession made for visitor appreciation was the placing of niches in several locations to accommodate electric lights.

The first step was dismantling the walls and relaying the masonry of the subterranean part of the edifice. That provided an opportunity to determine what was behind the last wall and thereby more definitely reconstruct the Great Kiva's history than had been done in the original excavation. The original bench facing, hidden beneath the veneer of a later bench, was found to be better quality and of more characteristically Chacoan masonry than the later bench placed there by people of the Mesa Verde occupation. A further clue to successive occupations of the building was noted in the remodeling of several of the floor features. There were obvious signs that the huge structure had suffered through several destructive fires. Courtesy University of Colorado Museum.

Rough stones, such as those littering the Great Kiva floor, were brought from excavated Anasazi villages on the La Plata River north of Farmington. They served as core filler for the restored walls. Most stones used in the veneer of rebuilt walls came from stockpiles set aside during the original excavations of the ruins. The reconstructed narrow, vertical wall slots with wooden rungs reached from the kiva bench top to the floor of peripheral ground-level antechambers. It is presumed that participants in rites prepared themselves and waited in these rooms for time to make proper entrance down the wall ladders. Courtesy University of Colorado Museum.

As the walls of the peripheral ground-level rooms began to take shape, Morris (in the center) discussed construction details with a workman. An unexcavated sector of the west wing appears behind them. Courtesy University of Colorado Museum.

Each of the four squared, sixteen-feet-high columns that had held up the roof were made up of courses of sandstone masonry interspersed with layers of peeled poles. When the kiva was first excavated, these had been seated in pits on four stacked, circular limestone discs approximately three feet in diameter. They provided a solid foundation to support the columns and the heavy load of the dirt-covered roof. Because of their great weight, they had not been raised during the 1921 excavations. But in order to rebuild the columns which rested upon them, a heavy-duty hoist was used to lift the stones from their original positions. The stack of discs had been centered in masonry-lined pits averaging four and a half feet in diameter. ▷ Stones were found to be tightly wedged in the space between the discs and the pit walls. Further, it was discovered that beneath the foundation stones there was a base deposit of adobe and lignite almost three feet deep. Morris reasoned that the original Chacoan Great Kiva had a roof support system of four huge logs that had been seated in the pits. They had burned at some time, to be replaced later by the Mesa Verdian columns. As he saw it, there had been two Great Kivas at Aztec, one within the remains of the other. Each had experienced some refurbishing during its existence.

△ National Park Service personnel observe the setting of the hoist over the seating pit associated with the western vault.

Above, right.
A view into one of the excavated seating pits shows its masonry lining, one of the set of discs in place, and the stones packed between the discs and the pit wall.

One of the heavy limestone discs, averaging about 375 pounds, is hoisted from its seating pit. ▷
   Photos courtesy University of Colorado Museum.

The four roof support columns, arranged in a square pattern on the kiva floor, had been only three and a half feet high when first discovered, but were estimated to have been some sixteen feet high originally in order to have supported a common roof over the kiva and its surrounding surface rooms. The subterranean wall of the kiva was about eight feet high and the ceilings of the attached ground-level rooms were judged also to have been about that height, as were the ceilings of domiciliary rooms in the pueblo. Morris reconstructed the massive columns with reinforced concrete, hiding it beneath a layer of plaster.

Wooden forms approximating the size of the original supports were put together across sawhorses on the kiva floor.

Here, one of the forms is in place and ready for pouring concrete into it.

Photos courtesy University of Colorado Museum.

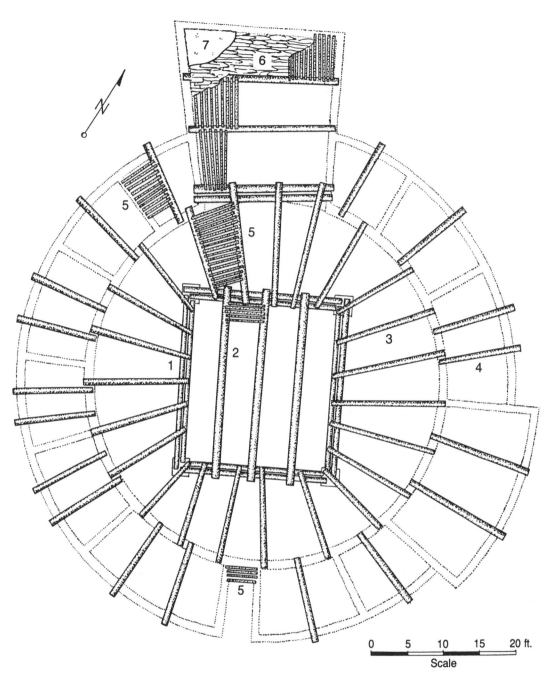

Probable plan of Great Kiva roof, as drawn by Morris in his report upon the excavation of the Great Kiva (Morris, 1921).

1. Large logs between tops of pillars.
2. Large logs resting on pillar logs.
3. Large logs radiating from pillar logs to peripheral room walls.
4. Large logs across peripheral room walls.
5. Small poles across large logs, between large logs and peripheral room walls, or across peripheral room walls.
6. Cedar splints on top of small poles.
7. Thick layer of dirt on top of splints.

A view from the northwest was taken when four wooden forms for the columns had been raised to roof height. The unfinished partition walls of the peripheral rooms spread out from the kiva core like spokes in a giant wheel. The straight wall at center is that of the rectangular projection from the circular building of the north alcove. Prepared logs to be used in roof construction lie in the foreground.

The first roof elements to be put in place were those spanning the walls of the ground-level antechambers. Later, they were held in place by additional courses of masonry. While masons continued laying walls, in the center men raised the ponderous bearing beam across the wide opening of the northern alcove. The four concrete support columns had been poured and stripped of their wooden forms.

Photos courtesy University of Colorado Museum.

Here the masonry walls of both the kiva and its encircling surface rooms have almost reached their final height. Roofing of the immense structure continues.

With the primary beams in place, a compact square of smaller poles was formed over the center of the kiva, running in opposite direction to that of the beams. Similar poles then were positioned between each of the radiating beams and those of the surface rooms.

Workers, here seen installing the pole layer, would then cap it with a thick stratum of juniper splints oriented in the same direction as the log beams. On top of that would go a foot-deep deposit of earth to make the uppermost roof covering. The estimated weight of the roof, which encompassed over 1800 square feet, was some ninety tons. It was a prodigious task to span such a large area and secure the roof in position without the benefit of nails, tenons, or pegs. The Anasazi architects of the Great Kiva were no less skilled than the archaeologist, shown at the far right, who faithfully duplicated their endeavor.

Photos courtesy University of Colorado Museum.

△

A ranger stands in the southern section of the kiva before the roof was finished. On the floor are the two vaults, two of the roof columns, some of the limestone discs taken from the column seating pits, and the fire box. The niches placed high on the columns were to accommodate electric lights for illuminating the kiva's interior. On the wall are ladder slots, entrances to peripheral rooms, and the stairway leading to the southern passage. Courtesy National Park Service.

In preparing materials for incorporation ▷ in the kiva roof, some men peeled small poles and cut them to proper length. These would comprise the secondary ceiling component above the square of primary beams resting on the masonry columns, on others radiating out from them, and on top of the stringers of the surface rooms.

Other workers split juniper shakes or ▷ splints, which would form a tightly packed layer above the poles.

Photos courtesy University of Colorado Museum.

A view looking north reveals the dirt floor, a corner of the central fire box, a segment of the western floor vault, one column with a cut-away section replicating its original masonry and pole construction, and a stairway to the northern alcove with its altar. The ceiling construction can be compared to that seen in the house blocks. Light enters the alcove through an east doorway to the plaza.

The interior of the Great Kiva was plastered with mud, as it had been when the Anasazi met there. Evidence was found for a red coating over the encircling bench and extending in a low band up the walls. Instead of using a simple red iron oxide wash that had the drawback of some impermanency, John Meem, a Santa Fe architect specializing in Puebloid style, furnished a formula for red plaster that consisted of reddish sand, hydrated lime, mineral red mortar color, burned umber, Vandyke brown, and raw sienna. The walls above were whitewashed.

Looking south from the ground level north alcove, the alcove altar is in the foreground. Beyond are the two west columns, a portion of a vault, the fire box, wall slot ladders leading to antechambers, and the south stairway.

Photos courtesy National Park Service.

The reconstructed Great Kiva stands serenely in the West Ruin plaza much as it did seven centuries ago.

The large south doorway and those of the peripheral ground-level rooms had been sealed by the second users, the thirteenth-century bearers of Mesa Verde culture, but the restorers chose to have them left open as they were built by Chaco occupants. The exterior was plastered once, as was the entire pueblo, but again the conservators decided to leave it unplastered, the way it and the remainder of the ruin were found upon excavation. Courtesy National Park Service.

△

This view of the northwestern portion of the Great Kiva shows the modern roof, roof drains, and skylight that were necessary additions for preservation and exhibition purposes. Courtesy University of Colorado Museum.

Looking across the courtyard from the northeast corner of the ruin reveals stabilized walls of the old pueblo, roofed Kiva E, the Great Kiva, and part of the unexcavated west wing. Courtesy National Park Service.

▽

At the very time the Aztec West Ruin was being exposed, a University of Arizona scientist, A. E. Douglass, was studying climatic fluctuations through time as reflected in the growth ring patterns of the Southwest's pine and fir trees. In the course of eighteen years of analysis, Douglass had found that by meticulously overlapping the patterns of annual growth rings revealed in cross sections of living trees and older beams that had been used in Spanish colonial churches, a succession of rings could be dated backward in time to the point when Europeans first arrived in the region. Douglass was not satisfied with that remarkable accomplishment. Knowing that Southwestern archaeologists were finding well preserved pine timbers in ruins they were investigating, he solicited their help. He felt that given the right specimens, the chronology could be extended deep into prehistory. Archaeologists would surely welcome calendar dates for their sites by which individual ruins could be placed into a regional sequence of cultural events.

As a result of all the publicity given Aztec's incredible ceilings and the other dangling beams that hung from its wall tops, Douglass came to the site in 1919 to ask for a sample of the construction wood. Together he and Morris designed a small boring tool that could extract a small plug from a timber without causing structural harm. Morris then supplied twenty-six samples from the beams of sixteen different rooms of the pueblo. These constituted the first prehistoric tree-ring lot to be subjected to dendrochronological scrutiny.

When the tree-ring report came back, it was learned that the Aztec beams had been cut only four decades after those in a similar sample taken from Pueblo Bonito in Chaco Canyon. That substantiated the presumed contemporaneity of the peak periods in the two areas but did nothing to pinpoint either of them on the Christian calendar. It yet remained impossible for Douglass to connect the sequence of relative dates derived from wood taken from the prehistoric sites to the more recent absolute series that yielded calendar dates. Ten years later, after juniper and charcoal also were proving usable, that hookup was achieved. Then it could be demonstrated that the cutting dates for the bulk of the West Ruin rafters were concentrated in a brief four-year span from A.D. 1111 to 1115, with a few beams dating at 1124. Assuming that neither earlier nor later beams had fallen victim to rot, fire, insects, or vandals, those dates indicated an astonishingly rapid construction of the great house. Considering that the ancient Pueblos lacked metal tools with which to cut timbers or break out and shape stone, wheeled conveyances or draft animals to transport materials from localities as much as twenty or thirty miles away, or mechanical devices such as winches, hoists, or compasses to lift materials and seat them properly, they accomplished an amazing feat in so hurriedly getting their carefully crafted Animas city ready for occupancy. The homogeneity and plan of the building and its seemingly fast erection implied a large measure of directive social structure, sheer human will, and backbreaking effort in its conception and completion. Although stunned at the relative recentness of the Anasazi developments as confirmed by the tree-ring dates, Morris was even more surprised at the compressed evolution which saw people transformed from living in pits in the ground to living in multilevel apartment houses such as that at Aztec probably within less than a millenium's time.

Quite surely some building continued through later years as the population grew or as the apparently insatiable remodeler's urge

had to be satisfied. It was unlikely that the first emptying of the town had taken place as soon as the last room was roofed, but just how much longer it may have been in use was speculation. Since the new dating data for Chaco Canyon suggested no further construction activity after about A.D. 1150, it was assumed that the parallel Chacoan structure at Aztec may have been occupied for no more than a half century, perhaps less. Therefore, in its own way, the rapidity of trash accumulation rivaled that of the builders, because when the last Chacoan family moved out of Aztec, the refuse heaps and litter in some rooms were head high.

A second grouping of tree-ring dates from roof beams at the West Ruin covered a forty-year period between A.D. 1220 and 1260, with a particularly notable emphasis on the years between 1225 and 1252. In the cultural sequence reconstructed from the excavation information, these years represented the Mesa Verdian rehabilitation of the structure. Again, those residents were likely to have lingered after building efforts ceased, perhaps until near the end of the thirteenth century when archaeological research elsewhere was showing that all the dwellers of the area's villages and towns had bowed under unknown pressures and departed the entire San Juan Basin. Even more than their predecessors, these residents left behind mountainous heaps of discarded material goods and many of their dead.

A 1929 photograph of a collection of
what Morris called Chacoesque pottery
from Aztec Ruins—as displayed when the
roofed rooms in the north wing of the
West Ruin were used as a museum for exhibiting some of the specimens recovered
from the site. Jars, bowls, pitchers, and
ladles are shown. Courtesy National Park
Service.

CHAPTER THREE

The Pueblo as Part of the Chaco Phenomenon

For seven hundred years Chaco Canyon had been the locale of an evolutionary sequence of Anasazi culture that resulted in a legacy of a dozen of the most awe inspiring aboriginal structures to be seen in North America. The West Ruin at Aztec, New Mexico, was conceded to have been a part of that cultural efflorescence as it reached a climax at just about the time Western Europeans were moving out of the Dark Ages. In the taxonomy of Southwestern archaeology, it was a time called Early Pueblo III, or part of the Great Pueblo period. The data available when West Ruin was excavated indicated only that it had been the residence of Chacoans forced by overpopulation out of the primary zone inhabited by their fellow Anasazi or of others destined to live on the peripheries of more consequential happenings at the cultural seat. It remained for recent intensive archaeological work in Chaco and its environs to provide a fresh provocative interpretation of Aztec's special role in the Anasazi world view.

For many years what seemed to be broad trails, or "race courses" as they were then called, were noted on some of the barren plateaus bounding the Chaco declivity or connecting important residential complexes in the inner canyon. With the aid of modern aerial imagery, these paths, often difficult to detect on the ground, were seen to interconnect at the canyon and could be followed outward for many miles. Up to twenty feet in width, often demarked by low lines of dry-laid walls of rocks and built up to grade, they spread like a spider web across miles of a bleak, craggy countryside that even today stretches to far horizons with few signs of human beings. Two main arteries were traced north and south, but dozens of segments of others went off in all directions.

Without animals to ride or carts to push, archaeologists postulated an Anasazi human parade trudging along these primitive avenues that both maintained a reciprocal flow of commodities essential for survival and a less tangible, interlaced network of social, economic, religious ties to bind the Chacoans together. One of these vital roadways linked Chaco Canyon with Chacoans dwelling on the San Juan drainage. During his researches at Aztec Ruins, Morris had noted a nearly three-mile stretch of road. He thought it may have been the route connecting a rock quarry to the building site. Although that may have been one use, the path very well could have tied into a roadway north out of Chaco to the recently excavated Salmon Ruin on the San Juan and then on to the larger, slightly more northeasterly West Ruin.

Behind the need for such a communication system, backed up by small way stations and a line-of-sight series of signaling stations, was the demanding environment in which the Chaco Anasazi had chosen to dwell. Now desolate with little native greenness in evidence at any season, in previous centuries the Chaco basin may have been a somewhat more benign land of grasslands, intermittent streams that had not yet cut themselves deep into the earth's crust, and a sparse covering of evergreens on high elevations. Nevertheless, it always was an agriculturally risky area unsuited to large-scale, unsophisticated exploitation. The thin soil was heavy with clays that forestalled permeability from the extremely variable rainfall that in some summers fell in sudden violent deluges and in others did not come at all. Early fall frosts and late spring freezes shortened the

months needed for maturing crops. Years of cutting building timbers and firewood denuded the hillsides to drive off the small game that had resided there.

As the population perversely continued to expand to include four hundred settlements in what actually was the least desirable sector of the eastern Colorado Plateau for agriculturalists, it became increasingly necessary for the settlers in the central area of Chaco Canyon to draw upon more plentiful resources from surrounding territories. There was considerable potential for procurement of an impressive range of commodities because of the ecological diversity of the expansive tablelands, mesas, and canyons adjacent to Chaco. Therefore, it is theorized that urgent need of various resources prompted the establishment during the eleventh and twelfth centuries of a string of outlying subsidiary settlements in varying microenvironments that in times of local stress could collectively provide the warehouses of the canyon with such things as foodstuffs, raw materials for handicrafts, and construction elements. These goods would have been moved over the roadways by teams of human carriers.

This system of exchange is not envisioned as having been a matter of tribute from colonies to a group of master communities but rather as an exchange arrangement which saw the central towns at the hub of the system supplying leaders and perhaps labor forces for needed far-flung projects, which seemingly included participation in an elaborate ceremonial cycle, in return for basic necessities. Now known to the scientific community as the Chaco Phenomenon, if it in fact had existed, it was a unique economic pattern born of adaptation to ecological restrictions that had ramifications in all aspects of Chacoan life. Its functioning and control surely culminated in an hierarchial structuring of the society. An elaborate water control system for floodwater farming, the road network, and signal stations are other indications of a strong leadership group in charge. At the same time, it is probable that the Chaco Canyon towns functioned as a center for redistributing needed foods, raw materials, and goods within its immediate sphere of influence.

Local and foreign resources and handcrafted essential and luxury items also were exchanged over a much larger area, perhaps as far away as outlying communities of Mesoamerican cultures in northern Mexico. Items recovered from excavations in Chaco sites, presumably of Mesoamerican derivation, include such exotic things as parrots and macaws, ornamental copper bells, trumpets and jewelry of shell, and certain kinds and styles of pottery objects. Several architectural elements, devices for water control, roads, signal stations, and means for recording astronomical data also may have come from contact with or diffusion from peoples to the south. One commodity likely traded by the Anasazi to folks in Mesoamerica was turquoise, the highly prized "green stone" of many of the more advanced cultures in that region.

So long as the managers and the managed worked together, it was a successful venture. Within a brief seventy-five years centering on A.D. 1100, there was a prosperous brilliant era at Chaco that never would be equaled in the prehistory of the northern Southwest. But the system's growing dependence upon products from afar and upon wholehearted allegiance and cooperation of men and women on the fringes of the Chacoan universe were fundamental flaws that, added to an unstable environment, quite possibly may have contributed to its rapid collapse.

If the notion is valid that workers were dispatched to the territorial frontiers to erect structures like those known at Chaco Canyon, that might explain the seemingly rapid four-year completion of the great house now called the Aztec West Ruin. It obviously was the workmanship of persons well versed in the architectural manifestations of Chaco Canyon's cities. This was typified by a multistoried complex of core and veneer masonry, spacious rooms, high ceilings, a central plaza, circular clan kivas, and the Great Kiva. The stone of the Animas valley was more difficult to work than the laminated sandstone characteristic of Chaco, but the same degree of variation is seen in other affiliated structures away from the canyon. The West Ruin was third in size of all known large Chaco houses, currently estimated to have from 405 to 450 rooms incorporating over 15,000 square yards of floor space. Only Chetro Ketl and Pueblo Bonito in the canyon proper contained more rooms and greater spatial extent. There is also the possibility that construction of a neighboring structure now known as the East Ruin may have commenced as the West Ruin was nearing completion, to be greatly expanded a century later by the incoming Mesa Verdians.

The question arises as to why such a hugh edifice was built away from the focal point of Chaco activity. The answer must be that the riparian woodland environment found along the Animas, its relatively more predictable rainfall, permanent waters, fertile soils, and its position near to timbered elevations with abundant game reserves made it a valuable breadbasket adjunct to the Chaco sphere. It is not unlikely that for a time its fields and those of the Salmon site and numerous small Chaco settlements in the vicinity produced surpluses of corn, beans, and squash, and the uplands were cut over for beams and hunted for small game that eventually got dispatched on the roadway to Chaco Canyon. Moreover, probably there were many successful harvests in other Chacoan towns now known north of the San Juan at Chimney Rock on the Piedra River, along La Plata River, and out in the red-soiled basin west of Mesa Verde which were funneled southward through Aztec. Some current studies suggest that

the West Ruin at Aztec and perhaps three edifices in Chaco of comparable grandeur (Chetro Ketl, Pueblo Bonito, and Peñasco Blanco) were administrative centers where a limited corps of elite persons was posted to maintain the roads and oversee the business of exchange. Unlike the sister cities in Chaco, the West Ruin sat in the midst of plenty. Many of the large rooms within the pueblo's matrix may have been depositories for goods in transit either to Chaco or to be redistributed along the road network or to more distant locales. If so, the West Ruin was extraordinary in being a bureaucratic establishment without common families eking out a living.

In addition to possible contributions of manpower, Chaco likely passed on to the San Juan some kinds of items not available in the immediate environs. Among these were macaw and parrot feathers, shell objects, and small copper bells that probably had been traded from some north Mexican entrepôt such as Casas Grandes, Chihuahua. From Southwestern places outside Chaco itself came cotton, salt, turquoise, obsidian, and some finished lithic implements and pottery vessels.

The known dates associated with the construction of the West Ruin also are of particular interest because they cluster so late in the lifespan of the Chaco Anasazi variant, which appears to have been dissipated by the latter quarter of the twelfth century. It has been suggested that as existence at the canyon became ever more precarious because of the failing regional economic system, sites founded along the San Juan drainage assumed greater power through greater productivity. One line of evidence is the increasing stylistic influence of the ceramics of that area on those at Chaco, accounting for the quality Morris had recognized as "Chacoesque." The success of the outliers on the San Juan and the Animas actually may have hastened the demise of authority at the culture's center.

It is ironic, however, that if the lowland on the Animas was selected as a contributory Chaco outpost because of its promising ecological attributes, it was a dream doomed to failure almost before it had a chance to prove itself. Within less than a decade after the last roof beam at the West Ruin was cut and put in place, the Colorado Plateau was experiencing another of its cyclic summer droughts, this one found to have persisted from A.D. 1130 to 1190. Most likely the Animas did not go dry, but over sixty years its flow at times may have dropped below a level at which irrigation canal intakes would have been effective. With insignificant summer rains and no river waters available, garden plots would have ceased to yield. Other settlements away from the river would have been affected more adversely. However, while demoralization from local crop losses undoubtedly was a contributing cause to the breakdown of the experimental Chacoan colonization north of the San Juan, the real lever to pry those migrants away must have been the deep rooted cultural and kinship ties to the more troubled populace at Chaco which was packing up and getting out. The Chaco Phenomenon was becoming the Chaco disaster.

Apparently the masonry in much of the West Ruin at Aztec was not as precisely or elaborately executed as that seen in the contemporary great houses of Chaco Canyon because the local sandstone did not fracture so neatly as that of the Chaco area. Nevertheless, there are examples of modified banded masonry, reminiscent of Chaco, wherein large loaf-shaped blocks alternated with several layers of thinner slabs. Attractive though the finished wall was, it aboriginally was thickly coated with mud plaster. Courtesy University of Colorado Museum.

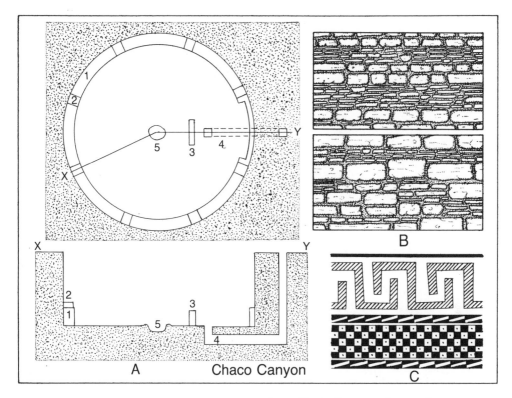

Some Chaco Canyon culture traits present at Aztec Ruins.

    A. Plan and profile of typical kiva.

        1. Bench

        2. Low pilaster

        3. Deflector

        4. Ventilator shaft

        5. Firepit

    B. Masonry types: banded and modified banded.

    C. Designs on black-on-white pottery: hachured and checkerboard elements.

Looking over the southeast corner of the West Ruin after the east wing, part of the three-story-high north wing, and a section of the south wing had been cleared. The latter arc of single-storied rooms had consisted of small, cobblestone-walled rooms that did not stand up well after abandonment, as may be noted in the foreground of this view. Their occupation is attributed to Mesa Verde people, the second residents of the site. Courtesy National Park Service.

CHAPTER FOUR

The Pueblo as Home to Mesa Verdians

The tops and escarpment faces of the Mesa Verde and a great expanse of land at its western foot had been densely occupied by the Anasazi since their earliest appearance at about the time of Christ. Of higher elevation than the valleys through which the San Juan coursed or the dreary plateaus that fell away to the south, these more northerly regions normally received greater precipitation from winter snow and summer rain. But the sixty-year drought in the twelfth century seems to have initiated a Mesa Verdian population shift that was to continue for a century.

A tide of Mesa Verde refugees had reached Chaco Canyon before the last of the original inhabitants had departed. Apparently the two groups lived side by side without conflict and shared many traits. However, the intruders from the north built four compact houses of pecked sandstone blocks set two courses thick rather than the core and veneer, massive-walled Chaco style. They also added on to some abandoned Chacoan structures using this same blocky masonry. Their diagnostic keyhole kivas were another intrusive feature. The Mesa Verdians continued to manufacture carbon painted ceramics, but not to the exclusion of some Chacoan mineral painted types. Although their inventory of other goods was limited, it seems likely they participated in some of the benefits of the Chaco Phenomenon and ultimately in its failure. By the early 1200s at the latest they were gone.

To judge from the protoclassic and classic pottery they discarded, at a more or less contemporary period to the move to Chaco Canyon another contingent of Mesa Verdians drifted southward down the La Plata River drainage that joins the San Juan at Farmington, but they continued to reside there after those at Chaco had gone elsewhere. The shallow La Plata valley was bordered by low, sage covered, flat-topped cliffs where many Anasazi before them had eked out an existence. The most recent had been some Chacoans who had erected two medium sized clusters of houses. The Mesa Verdians built shelters of their own over some of the more ancient sites and moved into unused Chaco buildings.

Still farther south in the San Juan valley itself and its northeasterly tributary Animas valley, the same pattern was repeated: build where necessary, remodel when possible. Because the number of people coming into the area was far greater than before, there was considerable new construction. The cobblestones that paved the valley terraces supplied the basic building material for modest-sized, carelessly constructed house complexes, as they had for those who built there before the Chacoans had arrived. One of these, now called the Old Fort, was at the confluence of the rivers.

The Aztec West Ruin was partially renovated, from which it was assumed that the Chacoans had departed before the Mesa Verdians arrived. If so, the cultural phase now termed Early Pueblo III had ended and Late Pueblo III was about to begin. In the course of making repairs to the West Ruin in the 1930s, buried Mesa Verde remains which correlated with the age of the Mesa Verdian occupation of Chaco Canyon were encountered. Therefore, the present evidence is that here too there probably had been some kind of joint tenancy for a time.

Although the American Museum of Natural History work at Aztec was concentrated upon the West Ruin, before the project terminated, it was necessary to probe neighboring structures in order to under-

stand their relationship to the larger site and to each other. Three such mounds were tested. An admittedly superficial examination suggests that all three mounds represented the Mesa Verdian occupation of the terrace. Apparently the West Ruin had been the principal twelfth-century Chacoan pueblo though it may have been erected on top of an earlier village whose residents were Pueblos sharing the common culture of the entire San Juan.

The most prominent of the nearby antiquities were two mounds collectively known as the East Ruin. The houses encompassed within those hillocks were by no means insignificant structures. Although no walls stuck up above the ground surface, the building encased in the easternmost prominence was at least two stories high in places and was estimated to have had from two to three hundred rooms. Its orientation and general plan appeared identical to that of the West Ruin. Morris recovered some Mesa Verde pottery and burials from several accessible rooms.

In 1957, thirty-five years after the museum project, additional work was carried out at the East Ruin incidental to a maintenance program. It was determined that many of the wooden elements in the East Ruin also had fortuitously survived seven centuries of neglect and that at least thirteen ground-level rooms at the western edge of the main mound still had their ceilings in place. The cellular architecture proved to be compatible to that regarded as Mesa Verdian in the West Ruin. This included rubble-cored walls double faced with pecked and smoothed tabular sandstone masonry and heavily spalled interstices, others of thickly mudded cobblestones, and some solely of adobe incorporating a few boulder inclusions. Plastered and painted walls also were common. Ceilings had been fashioned in the same manner as those at the West Ruin, but juniper beams outnumbered those of pine and fir. This may have been a result of the earlier builders having depleted the coniferous forest. The supporting beams for a balcony projection along the back, two-storied, north wall could be more easily observed at the East Ruin than in the West Ruin. The beams are dated to the twelfth century, which suggests they were reused. Another series of tree-ring dates from house beams were in the third decade of the thirteenth century. Although there were some signs of a Chacoan hand in their construction, the main body of evidence was that the East Ruin houses had been erected by colonists bearing a Mesa Verdian blend of the basic Anasazi culture at a time when portions of the West Ruin also were being refurbished by them and the West Annex was being raised. Such an opinion was reinforced by recovered pottery, half of which was classic period Mesa Verdian. Also present was a contemporary but limited amount of ceramics that the intervening years of research since Morris's day could more accurately ascribe to

other Anasazi markets. Contrary to the situation encountered just a few yards away at the West Ruin, the few rooms thus far examined in the East Ruin were not stuffed with rubbish or bodies. Apparently they were built and occupied as housing for a vigorous contingent of settlers who dumped their trash and buried their dead elsewhere.

Lying two hundred feet off the northwest corner of the West Ruin on an alluvial fan from the valley escarpment was another cobblestone and brush covered hillock known as the Hubbard Site. About 1918 five rooms on one flank had been cleared by the farmer owning the property and reroofed to serve as root cellars. In removing the aboriginal debris, fragments of Mesa Verde pottery had been found, as well as several flexed burials lying on the floors. In 1953 government archaeologists excavated the mound to prepare it for inclusion in the interpretive program of the monument. Their shovels uncovered three superimposed levels of occupation but all within the Mesa Verdian horizon at the Aztec sites. The first structures on this particular spot had been a few houses and a kiva with walls made of courses of puddled adobe reinforced by small poles. They were similar to what likely were contemporary shelters on the southern edge of the West Ruin. Found almost three feet below the final edifice at the Hubbard Site, the adobe still bore hand impressions of the builders, locked forever into their hardened earthen blotters. Above this partially eradicated complex was a somewhat later unit of sandstone masonry rooms, a kiva, and some stone lined, bottle-shaped, underground earth ovens whose walls were still reddened from old fires. This occupation unit, also containing Mesa Verde pottery, had been almost completely dismantled before a third and final building was raised on top of it.

It was this uppermost massive construction that was of most interest at the Hubbard Site. Believed to represent an architectural manifestation late in the history of the northern San Juan, it was made up of three concentric masonry walls enclosing a space approximately 64 feet in diameter. The walls were thought originally to have stood about twelve feet high. Spaces between them had been partitioned into twenty-two small rooms, the entrance to which presumably was through ceiling hatchways. A kiva had been sunk to a depth of three feet in the center of the enclosed circular court. Whether it had been roofed and how access might have been gained from the surrounding towerlike structure could not be determined. The kiva was not connected in any way to the encircling rooms. A smaller mound, Mound F, to the east of the West Ruin also contained a similar circular structure. In it and at the Hubbard Site, classic Mesa Verde pottery, other trade wares that were contemporary, and some flexed burials were unearthed. There was relatively little other material goods. As with the East Ruin, these circular build-ings definitely were not the scene of heavy trash disposal that the West Ruin had been in its final days. Ten double and tri-walled buildings of the same sort have been found in southern Colorado and northern New Mexico, including one in a Chaco site reused by Mesa Verdi-ans. Aztec Ruins is the only locality boasting two of them. Their function remains unclear, though some ceremonial purpose is probable despite obvious domestic usage. Also unknown is their relationship to other specialized circular buildings, namely kiva towers typical of the Mesa Verde domain or Great Kivas predominant in the Chacoan areas.

The probable reasons behind the second abandonment of the Animas sites are as mysterious as those behind the first. Enemies, exhaustion of natural resources, social decay, diseases, and internal strife have been suggested. But the most convincing argument was the farmers' constant foe, drought. Another devastating dry period occurred between A.D. 1276 and 1299 that climaxed what was all together an exceedingly arid century. Added to other troubles, it may have been too much.

Mass exodus of a people from a traditional homeland is a shattering event. However, archaeological research in the San Juan shows that periodic change of Anasazi home and farm sites was common. It was this kind of mobility that permitted fullest exploitation of a marginal environment. When flash floods wiped away top soil or the skies remained cloudless for days on end, a more favorable locale blessed with rain might be just over the horizon. Nevertheless, the scope of the final late-thirteenth-century flight had been unprecedented.

The Chaco and Mesa Verde Anasazi are thought to have continued their quest for a suitable new home until they reached other Pueblo Indians residing along the Rio Grande or near Zuni in New Mexico or about the Hopi mesas in north central Arizona. Their blood lines may well live on there, for their resiliency had been proven in a thousand years of coping with the San Juan country at places like the Aztec Ruins.

The Salmon Ruins is another major archaeological site in the northern San Juan Basin. Located on a terrace above the San Juan River near Bloomfield, New Mexico, it is only about ten miles from the Aztec Ruins. Extensive excavation of the site by Cynthia Irwin-Williams of the San Juan Valley Archaeological Project in the last decade revealed an E-shaped structure of approximately 175 rooms, originally two and possible three stories high in some sections, and a sequence of occupation that closely parallels that at Aztec. A primary Chacoan residency in the late 1000s and early 1100s is followed by a secondary Mesa verde period of tenure in the mid-1200s after a span of complete or partial abandonment.

Like the Aztec Ruins, the Salmon site, during its initial Chacoan occupation, has been included among the northern outliers of the widely extended Chaco Phenomenon. In fact, it likely was situated in a strategic position at the northern terminus of a major Chaco roadway extending to the San Juan River. Visitors to the Salmon Ruins will note many likenesses to the Aztec Ruins.

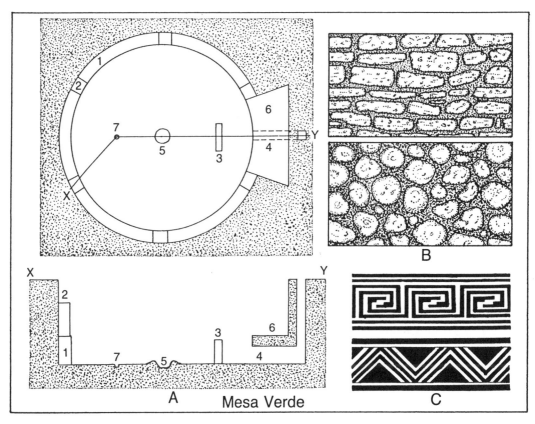

Some Mesa Verde culture traits present at
Aztec Ruins.

    A. Plan and profile of typical kiva.

        1. Bench
        2. High pilaster
        3. Deflector
        4. Ventilator shaft
        5. Firepit
        6. Southern recess
        7. Sipapu

    B. Masonry types: irregularly coursed
and cobblestone.

    C. Designs on black-on-white pottery:
interlocking frets and zigzag elements.

A

B

C

D

Additional vessels of typical Mesa Verde
black-on-white ware from Aztec Ruins.
Courtesy National Park Service.

◁ The single-handled mug was a form
unique to the Mesa Verde variant of San
Juan Anasazi culture. These, from the
West Ruin at Aztec, are two very fine examples of classic Mesa Verde black-on-
white ware and date to the thirteenth century. Courtesy National Park Service.

The Pueblo as Home to Mesa Verdians / 97

The Hubbard Mound to the northwest of the West Ruin was excavated by the National Park Service in 1953. It contained three levels of Mesa Verde occupation. Its most unique feature was a tri-walled circular structure around a central kiva. At present the site has been largely backfilled as a protective measure. Courtesy National Park Service.

CHAPTER FIVE
The Ruins Preserved

Once the protective layers of deposition are stripped from a ruin, it begins to fall apart and its characteristics get lost in the confusion of newly formed detritus. Very often the exposed fragile features of a ruin deteriorate rapidly through weathering.

Knowing this and wanting to prepare the Aztec Ruins for public exhibit, the American Museum of Natural History allowed funds and time for some cleanup and preservation measures to be carried out at the West Ruin while excavations proceeded. Since then this has become standard practice but at that time was a novel idea. The disposition of the enormous piles of dirt and rubble taken from rooms was troublesome because farm fields completely hemmed in the site. Morris was able to discard a lot of the spoil dirt in piles close to the ruin and had eighty-five wagon loads of it dumped to form a bed for a new road leading to the ruins. Fallen stones were stockpiled for repair work. Many of the high walls along the north wing were

taken down two courses and then reset and capped in cement. Some fallen walls were rebuilt to strengthen contiguous features. Such repairs were very obvious because the color of the cement was far different from the color of the original mud mortar. The capping of some wall tops was channeled to help carry water away from the facing and into the dirt plaza. To protect ten of the wooden ceilings, roofs of cement were poured over them which were not visible from below. Shortly after Morris left the project, a new caretaker made doorways out of the jagged holes the first explorers had punched through connecting walls in the north wing's ground level. While these steps helped curtail damage, they did not halt it, and the untreated sections of the site began to show threatening signs of giving way. The Great Kiva became an eyesore as its surface rooms and floor features crumbled. Anxious local citizens petitioned Congress for funds for immediate repair of the ruins in their backyard, which finally were alloted in 1933–34.

Recounting the work undertaken by the National Park Service illustrates not only the challenge of outsmarting the elements but also the enormous expense which, unlike the original excavation, is ongoing. Time had shown government engineers that Aztec Ruins, a place presumably deserted twice because of too little water, now was vulnerable to damage from a natural high watertable and from seepage from the irrigation ditch along its north side. Ground water had slowly oozed beneath portions of the great house and down the slight slope of the plaza to dampen the floors and lower walls of the clan kiva that Morris had excavated and reroofed in the plaza and the Great Kiva. The walls had been bone dry when excavated twelve years earlier. Also the soft sandstone used in the pueblo's construction was being attacked and disintegrated by capillary moisture.

The major portion of the federal monies went into a complete restoration of the Great Kiva. Morris, who was called in to supervise the work, meticulously checked plans against the archaeological record. The Aztec Great Kiva remains the only structure of its kind ever rebuilt and is the interpretive climax of a ruin tour. To carry off the subsurface water that was damaging the building, trenches up to 17-feet deep lined with tile drains were cut across the plaza to connect to drains from the roof of the Great Kiva. It was then that the earliest Mesa Verde structures were found.

Another aspect of the 1933–34 work was relaying the entire facing on the outer west wall and much of the exterior veneer of the north wall. Untinted cement continued to be used in this masonry work, but to make it less conspicuous, it was kept well back from the facing. Some of the 1920 cement work was redone in this technique. By the 1930s the emphasis in stabilization efforts had become one of making them appear as much like the aboriginal work as possible while imparting the strength of modern materials.

Two years later severe weather collapsed some walls and put wooden ceilings in jeopardy. The custodian hastily installed tar paper roofing over seven roofs because he felt the weight of the cement slabs formerly used was detrimental.

Shortly before World War II the National Park Service formed a unit headed by an archaeologist and staffed by specially trained Navajo Indians to deal with the growing problem of keeping the Southwestern ruins sound. Some stabilization was done at that time in the west wing of the West Ruin experimenting with new bituminum products which were waterproof and the color of adobe mud. Further maintenance work had to be suspended because of the war. Meanwhile the irrigation ditch continued to flow, water continued to seep into deeper structures, and foundations were becoming soaked through capillary action. Stopgap measures included installing pumps in kivas and digging wells in the plaza and outside the north wing in a fruitless effort to change the flow's direction away from the building. After the war, a 1000-foot-long tile drain was laid at a maximum depth of 22 feet along the exterior of the north wall. That satisfactorily took care of subsurface water and allowed the waterlogged ruin to dry out.

During the next forty years constant repairs of the ruins have been needed. The viewing public has been unaware of most of them. Large sections of the north and east room blocks have been repaired and stabilized, with a return to use of tinted cement as the most durable mortar. The cobblestone south wing had been backfilled after excavation, but under the National Park Service program it was reopened and refurbished with waterproof foundations, and three previously unexcavated rooms were dug. Other rooms were cleared as trails were established or damage seemed imminent.

Special efforts concentrated on the intact roofs in both the West and East Ruins, where weight of the cement slabs and leakage were causing some beams to bend and crack. After piecemeal applications of tar, sand, and earth failed to take care of the problem, there was no solution except to cautiously remove the old protective coverings and reroof the rooms using modern materials and methods. Often this involved getting rid of tons of overburden and tightening supporting walls. Today's visitors cannot see the layers of felt, tar, gravel, and metal drains, and the seven-hundred-year-old wooden elements are secure.

The tri-walled structure at the Hubbard Site was stabilized but has been partially backfilled as a protective measure. The open rooms with ceilings and the rooms Morris excavated in the East Ruin were repaired. However, for safety reasons this largely virgin ruin and the one containing the second tri-wall are not open to the public. The remainder of the mounds within the monument await further exploration.

Mother Morris, who came to the San Juan area and settled in Farmington in 1892, spent her adult life in the shadow of Southwestern antiquities. Her husband, Scott, was one of the first in the region to sell relics. He put the first exploratory trench in the great trash mound in front of Pueblo Bonito in Chaco Canyon and dug in numerous sites in the San Juan drainage. One was in the yard of a log cabin he had rented on the mesa overlooking Farmington. There his three-year-old son, Earl, unearthed a small pot and was forever after entranced by the Anasazi. That son went on to become the scientific excavator of Aztec Ruins in the first step of a long, productive archaeological career.

Mrs. Ettie Morris is shown here about 1920 standing in an excavated room in the west wing of the West Ruin. To her right a large corrugated pot had been found buried beneath the floor of the room. Courtesy University of Colorado Museum.

Morris was an avid collector of Anasazi ▷ pottery. The beginnings of his personal collection obtained from all parts of the San Juan Basin were displayed on one wall of the living room. At the time of his death in 1956, his collection contained 361 specimens, which were acquired by the University of Colorado. Courtesy University of Colorado Museum.

In 1919 and 1920 Morris constructed a three-room house in front of the south-west corner of the ruin compound, which he shared with his mother. By reusing building stones from the ruin and not hiding them beneath plaster, it blended in suitably with its backdrop. Only the porch was plastered with earth-tinted cement. Even a dark band of masonry, similar to those in the ancient pueblo, was placed on the facade of the house. Interior walls were covered with adobe mud and then whitewashed. Beams and poles in ceilings were slightly burned to give them the appearance of age. Courtesy National Park Service.

These three views of monument headquarters and visitor center show its
growth over the past half century. The
upper-left photo is a 1934 view of monument headquarters, originally the Morris
home, and a newly constructed restroom
building and parking lot. The modern
roof in the foreground covers several excavated rooms in the southwest corner of
the West Ruin. They were roofed in 1920
and used many years thereafter as a garage and blacksmith shop by American
Museum of Natural History and National
Park Service personnel. Courtesy National
Park Service.

◁ The headquarters and visitor center of Aztec Ruins National Monument, as it appeared about 1940, incorporates the
Morris house. The road leading to it goes
over tons of sterile overburden removed
from the west wing of the site. Courtesy
National Park Service.

In this 1986 view, additions to the build- △
ing for administrative and interpretive
purposes may be noted. More than
60,000 visitors now pass annually
through these gates. Courtesy Robert H.
Lister.

So much ground water seepage entered
Kiva E (which was repaired and reroofed
in 1916) that, even with a pump installed
in the ventilator shaft, the interior became
mouldy and five feet of soil around the
cribbed roofing stayed damp continually.
It was feared that the roof would rot. In
order to allow water standing on the floor
to evaporate, it finally became necessary
to remove the roof. A few logs were left in
place to illustrate the cribbing technique.
Courtesy Jerry Jacka © 1981.

Concurrent with the Great Kiva restoration, Morris supervised some further clearing of the west wing. A tremendous lot of fill and debris that covered the room block was removed by teams and wagons. Trenching was done to locate wall footings and rooms adjacent to the outer limits of the wing were cleared. The exterior wall of the wing, notable for two bands of four to five courses of dark green stones, was taken down and relaid. A few similar bands of the same stone appear in some interior room walls. The reason for this apparent decorative treatment is unclear inasmuch as the surfaces likely were plastered during the life of the pueblo.

Green stone bands appear in a room in ▷ the west wing. This photo was taken after the monument had been fenced and a roof, shown in the center, placed over several excavated rooms so that they could be used as a shop and garage. Courtesy National Park Service.

The short section of the west wing band △ depicted in this photograph shows that it was an integral part of the wall veneer. Courtesy Jerry Jacka © 1985.

Continuous on-going maintenance is an absolute necessity in a ruin such as Aztec, even though stabilization measures are performed during and after the site is excavated. These two sets of "before" and "after" photos illustrate the sort of routine problems that commonly arise and how they are resolved.

After an unusually wet winter one wall of the room above partially collapsed and the veneers of the others were damaged.

In restoration below, the collapsed wall was rebuilt and the sections of collapsed veneer were reseated.

Photos courtesy National Park Service.

This basal section of a room wall, which has a sealed doorway, shows how the soft sandstone construction blocks and the mortar and chinking in the joints deteriorate just above ground level. There, standing water from rains and melting snows is drawn into the wall through capillary action, washing away the mortar, loosening and causing the spalls to fall from the joints, and even somewhat dissolving the soft building stones.

The "after" view below shows how National Park Service stabilization and maintenance specialists have replaced the damaged stones, and repointed and replaced the spalls in the joints.

Photos courtesy National Park Service.

An aerial view, looking southeast, shows
part of Aztec Ruins National Monument.
Lower left, the Hubbard Mound; center,
the West Ruin; right, the visitor center;
top center, residences and utility area.
Courtesy National Park Service.

Recent examples of paintings and photographs add a human dimension to the
stark, long silent ruins at Aztec.

One example is an artist's conception for
the Visitor Center of an active pueblo
much like Aztec showing various activities
of life being carried on in the central
courtyard and on roof tops. At the West
Ruin there were a few doorways opening
into the plaza so that not all access to
surrounding rooms was through rooftop
hatchways. Most small clan kivas did not
stand so high above ground level as is
shown in this reconstruction. Courtesy
National Park Service.

The May, 1951 issue of *Arizona Highways* stated, ". . . we take a journey into many yesterdays ago, wherein we try to construct in word and picture the story of the prehistoric Southwest. . . ." Featured in the presentation were reproductions of paintings by internationally known author-artist Paul Coze of fourteen well known Southwestern ruins as they might have appeared when they were living entities. Aztec's Great Kiva was the featured painting. It was the two-page centerfold, depicting the beginning of a ceremony in the great community sanctuary as envisioned by Coze. A clown is shown dancing near a pile of vegetable offerings to the chant of a chorus; other dancers, awaiting their turn, and spectators look on from the dim background. Courtesy Southwest Parks and Monuments Association.

Renowned Southwestern photographer, Jerry Jacka, brought a touch of life to Aztec by posing a woman weaving a basket in a room. The line of rooms shown are in the northwest sector of the ruin, some of the ones first tunneled into by local citizens in 1881–82. The doorways are not original. The first modern entrants breached the walls in the photograph to gain access to the rooms and their contents. George L. Boundey, custodian of the monument in 1927, remodeled the irregular breaches into rectangular doorways and cleaned out the rooms to prepare them for a museum. Courtesy Jerry Jacka © 1985.

Another Jerry Jacka photograph recreates
a minor ceremony in the Great Kiva.
Courtesy Jerry Jacka © 1985.

Additional Readings

Irwin-Williams, Cynthia
1972 The Structure of Chacoan Society in the Northern Southwest, Investigations at the Salmon Site—1972. *Eastern New Mexico University Contributions in Anthropology,* No. 4, Portales, New Mexico.

Judge, W. James
1984 New Light on Chaco Canyon. In New Light on Chaco Canyon, edited by David G. Noble. *Exploration,* Annual Bulletin of the School of American Research, pp. 1–12, Santa Fe, New Mexico.

Judge, W. James, and John D. Schelberg (editors)
1984 Recent Research on Chaco Prehistory. *Reports of the Chaco Center,* No. 8, Division of Cultural Research, National Park Service, U.S. Department of the Interior, Albuquerque, New Mexico.

Lister, Florence C., and Robert H. Lister
1968 *Earl Morris and Southwestern Archaeology.* University of New Mexico Press, Albuquerque, New Mexico.

Lister, Robert H., and Florence C. Lister
1981 *Chaco Canyon, Archaeology and Archaeologists.* University of New Mexico Press, Albuquerque, New Mexico.
1983 *Those Who Came Before, Southwestern Archeology in the National Park System.* Southwest Parks and Monuments Association, Globe, Arizona.

Marshall, Michael P., John R. Stein, Richard W. Loose, and Judith E. Novotny
1979 *Anasazi Communities in the San Juan Basin.* Albuquerque Photo Lab., Inc., Albuquerque, New Mexico.

Morris, Earl H.
1919 The Aztec Ruin. *Anthropological Papers of the American Museum of Natural History,* Vol. 26, Pt. 1, New York.
1921 The House of the Great Kiva at the Aztec Ruin. *Anthropological Papers of the American Museum of Natural History,* Vol. 26, Pt. 2, New York.
1924a Burials in the Aztec Ruin. *Anthropological Papers of the American Museum of Natural*

History, Vol. 26, Pt. 3, New York.

1924b The Aztec Ruin Annex. *Anthropological Papers of the American Museum of Natural History,* Vol. 26, Pt. 4, New York.

1928 Notes on Excavations in the Aztec Ruin. *Anthropological Papers of the American Museum of Natural History,* Vol. 26, Pt. 5, New York.

Powers, Robert P.

1984 Outliers and Roads in the Chaco System. In New Light on Chaco Canyon, edited by David G. Noble. *Exploration,* Annual Bulletin of the School of American Research, pp. 45–58, Santa Fe, New Mexico.

Powers, Robert P., William B. Gillespie, and Stephen H. Lekson

1983 The Outlier Survey, A Regional View of Settlement in the San Juan Basin. *Reports of the Chaco Center,* No. 3, Division of Cultural Research, National Park Service, U.S. Department of the Interior, Albuquerque, New Mexico.

Richert, Roland

1964 Excavation of a Portion of the East Ruin, Aztec Ruins National Monument, New Mexico. *Southwestern Monuments Association, Technical Series,* No. 4, Globe, Arizona.

Schart, William L.

1977 *An Assessment of the Archeological Resources of Aztec Ruins National Monument, New Mexico.* Southwest Cultural Resources Center, Southwest Region, National Park Service, Santa Fe, New Mexico.

Vivian, Gordon, and Paul Reiter

1960 The Great Kivas of the Chaco Canyon and Their Relationships. *Monographs of the School of American Research and the Museum of New Mexico,* No. 22, Santa Fe, New Mexico.

Vivian, R. Gordon

1959 The Hubbard Site and Other Tri-Wall Structures in New Mexico and Colorado. *Archeological Research Series,* No. 5, National Park Service, U.S. Department of the Interior, Washington, D.C.

Wenger, Gilbert R.

1980 *The Story of Mesa Verde National Park.* Mesa Verde Museum Association, Inc., Mesa Verde National Park, Colorado.

Index